ATTENTION!

The Art of
Holding Your Audience
in the Palm of Your Hand

D1226168

Ajalon Publishing Co.
Ft. Thomas, KY 41075
www.sboyd.com

ATTENTION!

The Art of
Holding Your Audience
in the Palm of Your Hand

18 Strategies for Captivating Your Audience

Stephen D. Boyd, Ph.D.
Lanita Bradley Boyd

This book is dedicated to
our first audiences, our parents,
Paul and Dorothy Boyd
and
Lawrence and Mary Bradley;
to the many audiences that helped us
formulate and practice the ideas here;
and to our continuing and encouraging audience,
our children,
Josh and Gina Boyd
and
Kelsey and Stephen Byers.

Table of Contents

ABOUT THE AUTHORS

Steve Boyd has given entertaining yet thought-provoking after-dinner speeches ever since winning the International Toastmasters Speech Contest in 1970. He conducts workshops and seminars for national and international associations and businesses whose people want to speak and listen effectively and writes for trade magazines and journals. His previous books have sold over 30,000 copies. Steve earned his Ph.D. from the University of Illinois and is Professor of Communication in the College of Informatics at Northern Kentucky University. Steve has held the attention of college students for 40 years, plus delivering over 4000 speeches, seminars, and sermons during that time.

His wife Lanita Bradley Boyd taught public school for 34 years and now writes and speaks to women's and parenting groups. She has published in magazines such as *Woman's Day* and *The Lookout* and has personal experience stories in more than twenty books, among them *Chicken Soup for the Shopper's Soul* and *God Allows U-Turns.* She earned a Master's degree from Northern Kentucky University.

Their children also teach, speak, and write. Son Josh Boyd is associate professor at Purdue University and his wife Gina teaches gifted and talented elementary school students.

They have two children, Kinley and Knox, who do their own kinds of speaking and writing.

Daughter Kelsey Boyd Byers, former cover copy manager for Thomas Nelson Publishing, teaches ESL students and speaks to adoptive parenting groups. Her husband Stephen Byers an electrical engineer for Siemens Corp., keeps them all grounded.

Steve and Lanita live in Fort Thomas, Kentucky, near Cincinnati.

Attention: Key Factor in Effective Communication

If your efforts are sometimes greeted with indifference, don't lose heart. The sun puts on a wonderful show at daybreak, yet most of the people in the audience go on sleeping.
~Ada Teixeira

Poor attention permeates our culture. Distractions are a common problem and a major culprit is multi-tasking. According to the National Highway Traffic Safety Administration, "Multitasking drivers are three times as likely to be involved in an auto crash as more attentive motorists who don't dab on makeup, eat breakfast, or chat on cell phones." Emergency room physicians report a huge increase in face, chin, mouth, and eye injuries due to falls when people text message as they walk.

Routine affects your attention span. Have you ever driven such a familiar route that you arrive at your destination and don't remember how you got there? Frightening, isn't it? Our routine often hinders our attention.

And we humans have a problem paying attention, period. This can be seen in the story about the man who asked his friend, "Have you heard the story about the dirty window?"

"No, what is it?"

"Oh, well, you couldn't see through it anyway."

The next day the friend thought he would tell his neighbor the joke. So he asked, "Have you heard the story about the window you couldn't see through?"

"No," replied the neighbor. "How does it go?"

"Oh, well, it's too dirty to tell anyway."

> *The single greatest secret of success is paying attention.*

In our experience, the single greatest secret of success is paying attention. This is especially true in speaking. Anyone's attention span when listening to a presentation is very short. Since a speaker can be sure to lose the listener's attention several times, one of the speaker's main responsibilities is to keep bringing the audience's attention back to the presentation.

The typical length of speeches today is from 20 to 45 minutes. In the Lincoln Douglas debates of 1858, each side spoke for three hours; in the 2008 presidential debates, each candidate was given two minutes to respond to each of nine topics, with a five-minute discussion following each.

President's Barack Obama's inaugural address was 18 minutes in length, two-thirds as long as President Abraham Lincoln, and even farther removed from President William Henry Harrison's hour and 45 minutes.

Today's pervasive technology--making cell phones almost obsolete and with more gadgets added daily—can create a number of distractions for the listener during a presentation. When Steve first started speaking, his main distraction was an audience member reading a newspaper during his speech!

Today's problems are quite different. During a recent winter semester, a student announced in the middle of Steve's class that classes were dismissed because of the accumulation of snow. Since Steve had received no information from the main office during his lecture, he asked how the student knew: the student's friend had just texted him with the news.

This book focuses on how to develop winning presentations by getting and holding attention. Because we are exposed to so much information and because so many things demand our attention, we have a hard time attending to the important. As Yogi Berra said, "You can observe a lot just by watching." But to accomplish such, you must learn to pay attention.

ATTENTION!

To communicate better, you must pay attention to what is going on around you. One of the problems in listening to someone else is faking attention. We look at the person talking and even nod our heads at appropriate times, and yet our minds are somewhere else. How often have you suddenly realized that you have a great deal at stake in what someone is saying to you, yet you've missed some of it while looking at the speaker and appearing to be paying attention?

When conversing with another person, don't check email or respond to a message on your desk. We simply cannot pay attention and do other things without missing important aspects of human relationships. Recently, Steve went into a friend's office to chat for a few minutes. Even though his friend said, "Hello" in a friendly way, he continued to check and even answer his email. It was a short visit.

Apply self-discipline. Tune people in, don't tune people out. Don't make people feel like Jan Brady in "The Brady Bunch Movie" when she asked, "Don't I have a voice? Am I invisible?" If you don't have time to listen, admit it so you aren't rude to the other person. Make an appointment to listen at a later time.

When attending a meeting, volunteer to take notes; that will give you motivation to pay careful attention throughout. If you are going to be there anyway, taking notes will help you to become the best listener possible.

Listen to others as though you will ask a question about what they have said. Even if you don't ask the question, simply having the mindset for assimilating information to ask follow-up questions will heighten your attention skills.

Remove distractions when possible. Close the door to your office when concentration is critical, and don't answer the phone when people are in your office. Avoid important conversations when you or the person you are talking to is hungry or eager to leave for home. Provide an environment where paying attention is encouraged by circumstances and surroundings.

Learn to concentrate. Pick out an inanimate object or have a pen and paper in readiness before making a phone call. Look at it as you talk so you will not be distracted by people walking by or other noises. Take a moment to think about the topic before the meeting or phone call so you create the mindset to pay attention.

> *Today's pervasive technology can create a number of distractions for the listener during a presentation.*

Don't schedule every minute of the day. Have gaps in your appointments so you have time to respond to unexpected events that might sap your attention during the next appointment.

To make it easy for people to listen to you, start your conversation by stating what you want to talk about and stay on topic. Don't bring up extraneous materials or go off on a tangent. Show excitement in your tone of voice and have purposeful movement with your body as you speak. Look at the person as you speak. These are simple ways of encouraging people to pay attention to you.

Expand your interests; this will encourage you to give attention to a greater variety of things. Once you learn about something new, you give more attention when that subject matter is discussed or observed. If you have a new baby, you'll be more attentive to young children. If you learn to fish creeks, you will be more aware of streams of water along the highways. Once you see a red-tailed hawk on a fencepost, you'll keep watching for more. Study people to be more aware of how people respond when communicating. You'll be motivated to pay closer attention as you relate to people.

Although this chapter is an overview of attention in communication, this book will center on how to have a winning presentation through getting and holding the attention of the audience. As William James stated, "That which holds attention determines action." Even with great content in your presentation, if you can't get and hold the attention of the audience you will fail. Here you have key principles on how to attract and maintain interest. To be attentive in a conversation is one thing, but to be the center of interest of 30 or 1000 listeners is a different matter; that is the scope of this book.

Many of you grew up watching "Mister Rogers Neighborhood." Fred Rogers was the star and he was a master at paying attention to his audience, even through the television camera. As columnist Jack McKinney wrote, "He didn't rely on a flashy set or colorful graphics. His secret was his ability to focus gently and completely on whatever person or thing was before him." Patricia Madson said in *ImprovWisdom*, "Life is attention, and what we are attending to determines to a great extent how we experience the world." Mr. Rogers helped his young audience to pay attention by giving his complete attention to them.

We want to expand your view of presentation skills so you can pay attention to that next presentation—and be able to hold your audience in the palm of your hand.

Pay Attention to Preparation

When you are not practicing, remember,
someone somewhere is practicing...and when you meet
him [or her], he [or she] will win.
~Former Senator Bill Bradley

A s Dale Carnegie often said, "A speech well-prepared is nine-tenths delivered." This quotation points to the importance of careful preparation of your presentations. You can have a great topic, be speaking to an enthusiastic audience, be excited about your topic, and yet not be successful if you are not properly prepared. You must continually work to get better and that comes through practice and preparation, the first requirements of a good presentation. Even Tiger Woods continues to practice and take golf lessons. When a team is on a losing streak, the manager or coach will often say, "Well, we have to go back to the basics to start winning again."

One of the difficulties with preparation is that you may be hard-pressed to determine when you are really ready to speak. So often when he is coaching Steve will hear, "Well, I thought I was ready, but I wish I had prepared more." You cannot cram for a speech like you can for a test. You cannot fake a good presentation; preparation is a must.

> *Even Tiger Woods continues to practice and take golf lessons.*

A traditional story of how to be ready to speak in public concerns Athenian orator Demosthenes, who had his students practice public speaking by putting marbles in their mouths. They began with six marbles and each day would remove one as they spoke. Finally the day came when they were speaking with no marbles in their mouths. So the moral of the story is: "Now that you have lost all your marbles, you are ready to begin speaking in public."

How can you insure proper preparation before you speak? To keep from being rushed, you must start preparing well in advance of when the presentation is to be delivered. You spend time *perusing* and *pondering*.

Ideally, you should start this part several weeks before the speech is delivered. Look through magazines, trade journals, newspapers, and the internet for relevant materials. Ask associates for content ideas. This is not the time to be writing ideas down so much as it is locating available, recent, relevant, and appropriate material for your presentation. This stage of your preparation may help you to determine what direction to go with the structure and limitation of your topic. These are all a part of the *perusing*, where you are continually looking at a variety of avenues to find material, but you are not yet formulating specific ideas.

With *pondering* you simply think about your topic. Turn it over in your mind. Consider the topic as you are driving to your next appointment or walking the dog or enjoying a sunset. This portion does not have to be done at your desk; in fact you may find your mind functions better when you are not attached to a desk or office. Wait to actually write ideas on paper until you have thought about the speech for a while. Writing may actually stifle the creative process and limit your focus. So wait a few days before putting things on paper. As Voltaire said, "One always speaks badly when one has nothing to say."

As you write down ideas and arrange support, you will begin to structure your material. Structuring your presentation is covered in detail in Chapter 5, "Pay Attention to Organization."Once you have a pretty good idea of what you want to say, you are ready to practice—and practice is crucial. As Sam Duff former professional football player, said, "I love to play football on Sunday. In fact, I do that for nothing. They pay me for the practices during the week."

Practicing to get ready for the main event involves three steps.

First is the WALK THROUGH. In this session you get comfortable with the words and organization of your presentation as you say them aloud. Don't worry about how you deliver the material. In fact, you might even deliver your speech sitting at your desk. If certain words don't sound good together, or you stumble in moving from point to point, or the structure just doesn't feel right, now is the time to correct it. Time yourself to see if of the length of the presentation is generally within the given parameters. This is the place to cut out material if it takes too long or to add evidence if it is too short. Generally you will not need to add extra main points, but simply add more support and evidence for the weakest points if you have time.

> *Your preparation should include the WALK THROUGH,*
> *the DRIVE THROUGH, and*
> *the FLY THROUGH.*

Don't wait until late in your practices to add new material because your comfort level with the content may not be what it should be. Try to cut or add during or immediately after the walk-through session. This walk-through is vital because here is where you get a sense of what else is required to be ready for your presentation.

11

ATTENTION!

The second part of practice is the DRIVE THROUGH. In this session you give attention to how you are presenting the presentation. Just as in driving a car, you have to pay attention to your posture and where you have your hands and feet to travel safely to your destination. In this practice session, stand to deliver the presentation as you would in front of the live audience. In fact, practice the presentation in the room where you will speak if possible. Have someone sit in the room to give you feedback on any distracting mannerism or anything else that does not seem right. Practice with visuals if you are using them. Consider how you use gestures to reinforce or describe what you are talking about. Use the actual notes you plan to use in the presentation. How comfortable are you with them? Check on your posture as you practice. Can you take a step easily when you move from one point to another? Are you able to look at the imaginary audience, or do you have your nose stuck in your notes?

The drive-through portion of your practice may be done several times. Comfort with your content as well as the importance of the speaking occasion will determine how many times you practice the drive-through part. The key is to practice enough to get comfortable, but not so many times that you get tired of your material or that you memorize the content word for word.

The third and final portion of your practice is the FLY THROUGH. As in a plane, when you are going so fast that you don't get a chance to see everything, you just view the high points. The last time through, perhaps a short time before you give the presentation, you check the major points. Are your notes in order? Are your visuals in place? What questions do you anticipate the audience asking at the end of your presentation? Perhaps one section does not seem quite right, so you go over that part aloud again. You check a source just to make sure you have the correct statistics.

Remember that these are essential practice sessions. Consequently, if you don't practice thoroughly in a realistic setting, then your presentation to the specific audience will be one of your practices; you have too much at stake merely to present a practice session when you should be giving a polished professional presentation.

> *Wait to actually write ideas down on paper until you have thought about the speech for a while.*

When it's time for your actual speech, relax for a few moments and visualize effectively getting your ideas across to the specific audience. You might practice your opening lines, main points, and conclusion just to get into the flow of the speech. Check your appearance in the mirror and confidently

ATTENTION!

enter the room where you are to speak, assured that you are ready to deliver a carefully prepared presentation.

You can see that preparation is much more than simply thinking about what you are going to say. If you follow these suggestions, you can be confident that you will be successful with your presentation.

Pay Attention to Overcoming Stage Fright

I've never gotten over what they call stage fright. I go through it every show. I'm pretty concerned, I'm pretty much thinking about the show. I never get completely comfortable with it, and I don't let the people around me get comfortable with it, in that I remind them that it's a new crowd out there, it's a new audience, and they haven't seen us before. So it's got to be like the first time we go on.
~Elvis Presley

Public speaking gets lots of grief. In one of his monologues, Jerry Seinfeld said, "According to most studies, people's number one fear is public speaking. Number two is death. Death is number two. Does that sound right? This means to the average person, if you go to a funeral, you're better off in the casket than doing the eulogy."

Can you identify with these feelings? "His hands shook as he waited." "Her heart beat fast, and she felt as though it would pound out of her chest." "His stomach felt queasy, his mouth dry." Is this the description of a person preparing to go to the front lines of a battle? No, this the way some people feel immediately before getting up to deliver a presentation. It is called *speech fright,* or *stage fright,* or *communication apprehension*—that feeling of nervousness and confusion when one stands in front of an audience to deliver a speech.

Physical manifestations of stage fright may take a variety of forms. One person may perspire freely, while another's hands may shake. One person's mouth may get dry and another's voice may quaver. Your arms, legs, or face may be tense, or you may get clammy hands or a queasy stomach commonly known as "butterflies." These words from Earl Nightingale may describe you: "When you give a speech for the first time especially, you may feel like you are in the terminal stages of some type of tropical fever."

One important point to understand about speech fright is that this is normal and expected when you are delivering a presentation. Even after years of experience, Winston Churchill said that before giving a speech he felt as if there was a block of ice in the pit of his stomach.

Take comfort in the notion that symptoms often are not noticeable to the audience, no matter how severe they seem to you. How do you battle this obstacle that causes many to avoid delivering presentations altogether and others to experience sleeplessness the night before speaking?

As we talk about fighting this battle, understand that you don't want to eliminate stage fright or speech fright, but simply to control the excessive anxiety. As Neil Armstrong said, "I think we tried very hard not to be overconfident, because when you get overconfident, that's when something snaps up and bites you." A certain amount of nervousness is good for you—it keeps you sharp and on your toes. We see the same principle in *Moby Dick* when Herman Melville has Captain Ahab declaring, "I will have no man on my boat who does not fear a whale."

> *Even after years of experience, Winston Churchill said that before giving a speech he felt as if there was a block of ice in the pit of his stomach.*

Here are some ways to pay attention to stage fright by learning to control it.

Be well prepared. Careful preparation of your presentation will increase your self-confidence level. Practice your presentation. Be familiar with your notes. Work with your speech until you feel comfortable with your content.

A manifestation of Lanita's stage fright is when she gets too emotionally involved in her topic and begins to get teary. Before one speech, her mother introduced her, starting her remarks with the day Lanita was born. By the time the introduction was over, Lanita was so mortified and angry that she gave her speech without a thought of a tear. From this experience, she learned to focus on something that irritates her so she doesn't get as emotional about a story she's telling.

Pause before beginning your presentation. Stand before your audience for a few seconds, look at them, and give them a chance to look at you. Pick out a friendly face or two. Often we pick out the face of the one who looks as though he or she would rather be anywhere but here listening to us. This can cause more anxiety. When you concentrate on friendly faces, however, you gain confidence, and as a result, you'll find more friendly faces to focus on.

Work especially hard on your introduction. Make it attention-getting, thought-provoking, and creative. Know your introduction thoroughly. Practice the beginning over and over. Make your first sentence count. Draw in the audience with your first words. Give direction to your audience early in your talk. Getting off to a good start and winning the audience over is an effective way to ease the tension you may feel.

Incorporate movement early in your presentation. Building in gestures to reinforce an idea or to help describe a scene in a story or illustration will help relax you physically and aid in the effectiveness of your presentation. An appropriate prop to get the attention of the audience will require movement of your hands and arms and take the attention away from you, which can help relax you as well. Make yourself do something by taking a step, changing facial expressions, moving your hands, or nodding your head to add movement to your presentation. One precaution: Make sure the movement adds something to your speech.

Don't take yourself or your presentation too seriously. A speech, good or bad, is not going to make you company president or company dolt. It is not the end of the world if things go poorly. As Mark Twain said about audiences, "They don't expect much." That may be a little flippant, but the point is a good one: if your listeners take away one idea from your speech, you have been successful. They won't recall the flubs you remember vividly.

> *Make your first*
> *sentence count.*

Develop a positive mental attitude about your presentation. Often the opposite happens. The closer the time comes to giving your speech, the more negative you feel about it and the people who will be listening to you. Train your mind to think positively when you begin to feel negative. Say to yourself, "I'm prepared for this speech." "What I have to say is important for this audience." "They will take away good ideas." "We are going to learn and have fun doing it." You can't think a negative thought and a positive thought at the same time. A positive attitude helps you take control of the situation from the beginning.

One fear in the back of every speaker's mind—unless you are speaking from a manuscript—is that you will have a mental block. What do you do when you forget in the middle of a presentation? If you have speaking notes and they are well organized, it is a simple matter to look at them and quickly find your place.

What happens if you have already panicked and looking at your notes doesn't help? The best bet is quickly to admit to your audience, "Sorry, I've lost my place. Give me a minute to find my train of thought." Then do whatever is necessary to get back on track. But whatever you do, don't fake it—your audience will never forgive you.

Having a mental block is not a problem if you handle it in the right way. In fact, this stoppage can help build rapport with the people in the audience, who probably will be thinking "this could happen to me" and will be pulling for you to find your place and continue your speech.

Another way to feel confident is to dress like a "10." Feel good about yourself by what you wear. Only wear clothes that make you feel like a "10" instead of a "5" or "6." This is not based on what you pay for the clothing, but rather how you feel when you are wearing these clothes. You may feel like a "10" in them because of the color or feel of the material or the way they fit your body. If you feel good about yourself then you will be more likely to feel good about your speech and the audience to which you are speaking.

One last point: take good care of your body before you speak. Get enough sleep, eat the right kinds of food, don't load up on caffeine, and leave off the desserts. Keep hydrated. Drink water before you speak.

Don't run from the battle. Face it. Use stage fright as a speaking tool. Control your excessive anxiety and you will find delivering presentations a positive experience; your presentation will enhance your image and make you a more significant contributor to your organization.

Pay Attention to the Audience

Never speak on a subject about which your audience knows more than you do.
~Margaret Thatcher

O ne of the first things we can do to improve our speaking skills is to consider the audience in our preparation. The better we know our audiences, the more effective we will be as speakers. We want to become *audience-centered* in our speaking. Alan Alda in his autobiography *Never Have Your Dog Stuffed*, tells the story of not regarding his audience when speaking to the Illinois State Legislature. He was asked to say a few words and ignored his preliminary information that many in his audience did not support his position on the Equal Rights Amendment. Even the consultant he was working with told him absolutely not to talk about the ERA.

He got carried away and did not read his audience well; he got off his topic and on to the ERA. His listeners began heckling him so much that the consultant crawled on her hands and knees to a place behind the podium, pulled on his pant leg to get his attention, and said, "Let's get out of here!" He finished a sentence or two and was almost attacked as he made his way out of the assembly. He did not consider his audience and bombed. He ignored Lord Chesterfield's admonition that "You must look into people, as well as at them."

Learn all you can about the audience as you are preparing your speech. Talk to the person who is responsible for your speaking. He or she will have a vested interest in your doing well and so will usually give you all the information you want. If possible, talk to people who will be in the audience. Learn about their concerns. Ask about buzz words or special topics unique to that organization. Go online and check out their websites.

> *Get to the meeting early and sit in the audience prior to your presentation.*

Google key people in the organization and see what you can find that might help you adapt your material to this audience. Perhaps talk to a previous speaker at the event. Find out his or her reaction to the audience when they spoke. If possible, get to the meeting early and sit in the audience prior to your presentation. That will give you a feel for the group and you may pick up on something you can mention in your speech.

Also learn as much as you can about the occasion and the circumstances surrounding the speech. What kind of room will you be in? How many will be in the audience? What are their expectations? How long should you talk? You can usually learn this from the person in charge of the program.

You also might identify the "elephant in the room at the beginning of your presentation. A bestselling book, *The Last Lecture,* is the text of Randy Pausch's final lecture at Carnegie Mellon University. Because of Pausch's eloquence even though he was dying of cancer, the lecture became one of the most viewed items on the Internet. At the beginning of the lecture he identified the "elephant in the room"—his terminal cancer. He spoke of what everyone in the audience was thinking about and with humor put everyone at ease; then he went into his speech about achieving childhood dreams. The audience could concentrate on the topic because of his self-disclosure.

You have a hard time doing all of this if you are a novice speaker because your main concern may be getting through the presentation without passing out. But at some point this will change. As you go from being a novice speaker to an experienced and effective speaker, these audience concerns will more and more be your focus. One does not simply arrive at that point because he or she has spoken a magical number of times. To say you have delivered 50 speeches does not necessarily mean you have become an effective speaker. We believe in one major criterion for effectiveness: when you are more *audience-centered* than "*self-centered.*"

In our early speeches we are self-centered. We worry about our speech being too short or too long. We are concerned about our appearance. Will this suit or slacks be appropriate for this group? The new speaker thinks about the things which can go wrong with the content or delivery of the presentation. But after a while we begin somewhat to enjoy the adrenalin rush we get as we go to the front of the room to speak. Next perhaps we do not rely on our notes as much and give more eye contact to the audience. We think more about the ways we discussed earlier of learning about the audience.

> "*You want your audience to say: 'Me, too,' not 'So what?'*"
> ~ Jim Rohn

But we really reach the effective speaker range when in each presentation our major concern is the audience. Will they understand? Is this material that will help them improve or be persuaded? What questions will they want answered?

Which terms need to be defined and explained as I speak? What will they do as a result of my presentation? How can this material keep them engaged throughout the presentation? How much evidence will I need to convince the people in this audience?

As time goes by, we become more expert in what we speak about and become more adept in delivering that information. We need to think about our audience in order to know what to leave out because we have so much material to choose from. A key way of limiting our material is to determine what our listeners already know and thus what additional information they need to hear from us on the subject.

Even if we deliver a similar speech from time to time, each presentation is different because each audience is different; our major concern is to influence that specific audience. We begin to make sure that for each new audience we have content that just fits that situation. Having this attitude keeps our material fresh because even though we are familiar with the speech, we realize our audience is hearing the information for the very first time!

Another approach to be audience-centered is to find ways to become a part of the audience. As Jim Rohn says, "You want your audience to say: 'Me, too,' not 'So what?'" Connect with the audience. Find something specific that you can say that puts you in the audience's place. You may refer to the bad weather in coming to the meeting by saying, "I know we all had some challenges coming to this gathering on the snow-covered roads." Or if you are similar in age to most of the audience, you say, "As baby boomers we all remember when television became a part of our family life." You are now concerned about your audience and forgetting self.

Once you get to the point of being audience-centered you will adapt more to the audience as you speak as well as in your preparation. If you are audience-centered and not self-centered, when you notice a person looking disinterested you can speed up your rate or vary your volume to bring the attention back to you. If you see a quizzical look among some in the audience, back up and explain your point another way. When you see shifting of weight and lots of movement of legs and arms, you cut your presentation short because you see they want the speech to end.

> *"I couldn't have completed law school without back channeling. We would ask each other questions and respond in ways that helped me understand the point the professor was making."*

One audience function that is a result of advanced technology is back channeling. This is the practice of electronically passing notes among some or all of the audience members during the speech. Twitter is a common back channeling device although any chat room-style application, such as AOL Instant Messenger, works. The general goal of back channeling is for the audience to assimilate and share information with each other about your presentation. People will be more actively involved and are less likely to fall asleep. Often they will give immediate feedback.

As questions arise based on interactive discussions online, you can respond to specific concerns. A strategy for easing into back channeling is to have someone monitor the back channel and interrupt you if there are any questions or comments that need to be addressed. You can also take a Twitter break—say simply, "I know you've been Tweeting about this topic. Let's have some open discussion now. What are you thinking or what are your questions?" An adjustment you might consider is to allow back channeling for certain parts of your program and curtail the use when you feel you need the full attention of the audience.

Technology has been a viable addition to the presenter for years. Now, with back channeling, technology is also useful for audience response during the presentation. A graduate of the Chase College of Law said, "I couldn't have completed law school without back channeling. We would ask each other questions and respond in ways that helped me understand the point the professor was making." One factor that the speaker has to get used to is less eye contact with the audience as they look down at their screens. As you get accustomed to this additional audience factor; these suggestions should help you to use it to advantage.

You don't just prepare your presentation, you prepare for your audience. You can't do one without the other if you want to be an effective speaker. Pay attention to your audience.

Pay Attention to Organization

Order is heaven's first law.
~Alexander Pope

C lear organization in a presentation is crucial from beginning to end. Too many points can leave the audience confused and weary. If we do not show clear structure in the opening, the audience will soon stop listening. We must be aware that when we start our presentation the audience is immediately concerned with where we are going in our speech. If that is not clear in the first two minutes, attention will wane.

Reveal the structure of your presentation at the beginning. Tell the audience in the first minutes how many points you will present. Preview them and then occasionally summarize what you have said. You rely on maps from your GPS, AAA Triptiks, Yahoo, or MapQuest to keep you going in the right direction. You get lost quickly without these when you are in unfamiliar territory. Remember that the audience can feel the same confusion if it does not know where you are going. Quickly give them a roadmap of what you plan to do in the presentation and then summarize occasionally to reassure them that you are still on track. As Lewis Carroll had the Cheshire Cat say to Alice: "If you don't know where you are going, any road will get you there."

Divide your speech into introduction, body, and conclusion. In the introduction, besides previewing your speech, you must get their attention with a story, question, startling statement, or humor.

> *Quickly give them a roadmap of what you plan to do in the presentation and then summarize occasionally to reassure them that you are still on track.*

The body of your presentation is where you spend the major part of your speech. Develop two or three main points in the heart of your presentation. Each point should be followed by supporting material such as stories, statistics, case studies, or analogies.

Although no specific number is exactly right, the number three seems to work best. Three points, three statistics, three instances are often the number you need to prove or illustrate a point. Of course if the point does not need lots of explanation, then fewer support items may work fine.

Above all, do not have too many points! When Woodrow Wilson touted his so-called "14 Points for Peace" in 1918, French Prime Minister George Clemenceau said of the points, "Even the good Lord contented himself with only 10 commandments and we should not try to improve on them."

In fact, the number three fascinated people throughout the centuries. So when you are thinking of the number of specific instances or statistics to deliver at one time, consider dividing them into groups of threes. Notice how people are geared to the number three. Three strikes in baseball and the batter is out. Children's stories are often grouped in threes: three pigs, three bears, three blind mice, three kittens who lost their mittens. We divide our day in into three parts: morning, noon, and night. A presentation should contain an introduction, body, and conclusion. You start a race by saying, "Get ready, get set, go!"

In his 2009 Inaugural Address, President Barack Obama at least ten times spoke in groups of threes, such as "...humbled by the task before us, grateful for the trust you have bestowed, mindful of the sacrifices borne by our ancestors," and "Homes have been lost; jobs shed; businesses shuttered." As other outstanding speakers do, capitalize on the human tendency to respond to the number three.

The conclusion should include a summary, a move to action step, or both. If you are delivering a persuasive speech, you might summarize your main points and then leave the audience with a statement of exactly what you want them to do. The conclusion should be short—no more than two minutes—and you should not include new material here.

> *The number three has fascinated people throughout the centuries.*

Because people remember best what you say last, you may consider an exit line after you summarize or move to action. An exit line is simply an appropriate quotation, testimonial, or your own pearl of wisdom that earns you the right to sit down. This keeps you from being tempted to end with a weak, "Thank you very much..." or "I guess that's about it...."

Another part of organization is the use of transitions to connect various parts of the speech. The best transitions are signposts which are numbering your main points: first, second, third. Internal summaries are also very effective and simple to use. You summarize your last point and then preview what comes next. You might say, "Now that we have talked about conclusions, let's move on to transitions."

A third type of transition is the interjection. This is a way of singling out a point you are making. "Now you may forget everything else I say this afternoon, but remember this one point," is an example of an interjection. Another might be, "Underline this in your notes," or "Put a star by this next point." This transition also helps bring the attention of the audience back to you the speaker.

One simple organizational technique is repetition. When listening, an audience cannot review your material unless you do it for them. In a book, we can go back and reread a chapter or page to make sure we understand. The listener can't do that, so with important points repetition is

> *When you are thinking of the number of specific instances or statistics to deliver at one time, consider dividing them into groups of threes.*

crucial. Repetition also helps remind the listener of the structure of your speech during the presentation. Putting an emphasis on transitions helps you eliminate meaningless expressions such as "OK," "You know," or "All right." You will also be less likely to include verbalized pauses, such as "Uh-h-h," or "Oh, um-m-m…," which make you appear uncertain or nervous.

All of the structure should be centered on a main point that can be expressed in a thesis sentence. Before you get too far in your speech preparation, write a draft of a thesis—the essence of your talk in one sentence. This may change as you progress in your preparation, but having this main thought in your mind will encourage you to avoid getting off your topic. Any support you develop can be clarified by asking yourself, "Does this relate to my main idea?" Thus you will be less likely to include material which does not support the topic of your speech and you will not go off on a tangent while speaking.

Another way to stress organization is nonverbally. When you move from one point to another, take a step away from the lectern. Move back to the lectern when you finish the point or story.

> *A thesis sentence gives the essence of your talk in one sentence.*

Change your tone of voice when you are showing the organization of your speech. Punch out your next point. Put vocal emphasis on a transition, or pause before you mention the next point. Hold up the number of your point with your fingers if you use the signpost approach.

ATTENTION!

Many aspects of speaking will contribute to your success, but nothing is more basic or will mean more to your effectiveness than careful organization. Take the time to provide structure to your presentation. Audience members respond well to structure and will overlook other weaknesses if your speech allows them to follow your material easily.

Pay Attention to Opening and Closing

Never be afraid to try something new. Remember amateurs built the ark—professionals built the Titanic.

"I feel so miserable without you, it's almost like having you here."

Just as this comment by Stephen Bishop caught your attention, so will a strong beginning and a strong ending enhance your presentation by catching the audience's attention. People remember best what you say first and last.

Whatever you do to begin, it must be something to gain the attention of the audience. One way is to begin with a story. People can't resist good stories. Another way of getting attention is to give a startling statement or statistic. A quotation is a good way to begin. Steve has begun a speech on the importance of speaking skills with a quotation from Dale Carnegie "Leadership gravitates to the person who can speak effectively."

Asking a question is an attention-grabber that makes everyone think and focuses the attention on the content of your question. Using a piece of humor relevant to your topic can also be a good way to get attention. Finally, you might get attention with a prop or a visual aid. Seeing a concrete object helps the audience to focus on you.

A second important part of your opening is to let the audience know what you are going to be talking about. You might say, "I'm going to cover three points in my speech, and they are…." Or you could state the purpose of your speech as an orientation. A good start will include getting the audience's attention and then providing a preview of the content of your presentation. Make sure your opening words count. Don't talk about the weather or how glad you are to be there to speak. Your first sentence should grab the attention and make the audience want to listen to you.

> *An audience remembers best what you say first and last.*

Usually an audience will give the speaker about two minutes to prove he or she is worth listening to. If your opening does not demonstrate significance, you have basically lost the audience for the rest of the speech. Using an attention-getting device and previewing your content will ensure that your audience will stay with you through the speech.

The opening and closing stand out when you use your uniqueness. This is a great place to help your audience separate you from all other speakers.

For example, when one CEO was speaking to a group of national journalists, he began by reminding them of how long they had known him and that they had written articles about him for the past twenty years. He then proceeded to quote adjectives they had used to describe him in their articles during his career as an executive. The variety of negative adjectives they had used indicated that they had often been very critical of him.

> *An audience will give the speaker about two minutes to prove he or she is worth listening to.*

This was a clever way for him to acknowledge that he had been a controversial person in the media. He ended the point by saying that that was the nature of his position, and then proceeded with the rest of his presentation. He demonstrated that he had done his home work on the audience and was able to laugh about the criticisms made about him; in so doing, he made the people who had written the negative information feel more comfortable as audience members facing the object of their criticism. This personal experience story was powerful because he had done his homework on his audience and uniquely put the data together for a story to get their attention.

Think about what speakers typically do in the type of presentation you are developing, and then do something different. A friend of ours, the CEO for a girls' dress manufacturing company, was to keynote their annual sales meeting. That year they had bought hundreds of yards of black and yellow plaid material for girls' dresses and few stores had ordered the dress. The fabric was a bomb; they had multitudes of little unsalable dresses made from this material and hundreds of extra yards of the fabric.

> *Use your uniqueness to engage your audience.*

For his keynote presentation, he had a suit tailored from this fabric and wore it on stage for his speech. The audience of company sales people immediately started laughing and clapping. The CEO was able to show immediately that he could poke fun at himself and the executive staff who had made the fabric-buying decision. He used this prop to segue into how things would be different for the upcoming year. He was using a unique approach—he was doing something different and appealing. Equally important is the conclusion. What you say last should give the audience something to think about and leave them with a positive impression of you and your speech. Don't end with a weak "Well, that's about it," or "That's all." Too many speakers end in something of a daze by mumbling, "Well, that's all and I'll be glad to answer any questions." Such endings may remind us of T. S. Eliot's phrase "ending not with a bang but a whimper."

> *When you do say "In conclusion…," make sure you are ready to conclude.*

Your last words should be food for thought or a move to action statement. Certainly you can summarize what you have said, but that should not be your ending. If you are delivering an informative presentation, you might end with an exit line such as a quotation that encapsulates your message. If the content is persuasive, you might end with a testimonial from a person the audience respects, emphasizing your point in a different way. For example, in a presentation on listening, Steve sometimes ends with the answer given by the CEO of a Fortune 500 company to the question, "What is the key to your success?" The executive's response: "I am a good listener."

If you want your audience to take specific action after hearing you, then you would say, "What I want you to do as a result of my presentation is…" You may not want to say it as bluntly as that, but you clearly want to stress what you want them to do as a result of your speech.

When you do say "In conclusion…," make sure you are ready to conclude. Don't still be speaking five minutes later. At this point you should be moving immediately to your summary and exit line or move-to-action statement. Too often speakers have trouble concluding and will say a second time that they are going to conclude.

> *Be sure to look directly at your audience as you say your first words and your last words.*

End with a flourish. Don't trail off as you conclude. If you have a good closing quotation or move-to-action step, you will feel confident and thus have an assertive delivery and positive manner as you end.

In either beginning or ending, be sure to look directly at your audience as you say your first words and your last words. Don't be getting your notes spread out as you begin or be collecting your notes and moving away from the lectern as you finish. Because the beginning and ending are so important, it is imperative that you have your notes in place and have a visual contact with your audience by looking up and at specific people as you say those opening or closing words.

Certainly the body of the presentation is the bulk of your presentation, and this is where you want to develop your reasons and evidence. To make sure the audience gets the most from your body, however, you want not only to get off to a good start but also to end with powerful and memorable words.

The commercials we remember are the ones that are different, unique, out of the ordinary. We remember movies that develop the plot in unusual ways. Houses that are not of the cookie-cutter variety attract attention. In like manner, your next presentation will stand out and be remembered better if you work to put your unique stamp on the opening and closing.

Pay Attention to Stories

**The destiny of the world is determined less by
the battles that are lost and won
than by the stories it loves and believes in.
~Harold Goddard**

The night was cold and dark and the traffic had been unbelievable. "I think I'd better call Mother and tell her we'll be late," I said to Steve. Since this was long before cell phones, he pulled off at the next exit and found a pay phone.

Then I panicked. "I'm not sure I remember their new number correctly!" Well, I thought, I have some change and a phone, so I might as well give it my best shot.

The phone rang and I held my breath. But an unfamiliar voice answered the phone.

"Is this the Lawrence Bradley residence?" I asked meekly, fairly certain of the negative answer. But I got even more than that.

"Naw, this ain't the Bradleys' house. But I know La'r'nce and Mary. You tryin' to reach 'em?"

44

With a sign of relief, I explained to him that I'd just used my last bit of change to call him, and that I needed to let Mother and Daddy know we wouldn't be there in time for supper.

"Hey, that's no problem!" he responded cheerfully. "I'll just call 'em and give 'em the message. What'd you say your name is?"

"Oh, I'm their only daughter!" I exclaimed. "Just tell them their daughter is on her way home for Christmas, but she'll be a little late." He agreed and we hung up.

When I got in the car, Steve looked at me expectantly. "Well?" he asked.

"I learned something about Southern hospitality just now," I told him. "It even extends to helping people who call your house as a wrong number!"

Lanita tells this story as support for the point that Southerners continually set the standard and validate their reputation for being hospitable. To be effective as a speaker, we must tell stories; stories communicate layers of meaning and touch feelings. People can't resist a good story, just as in childhood. Some of our favorite memories come from stories such as "Cinderella" and "Snow White and the Seven Dwarfs." Many outstanding speakers of the past, from Jesus Christ to Abraham Lincoln have relied on stories to carry their messages. Great speeches such as R. H. Conwell's *Acres of*

ATTENTION!

Diamonds have been passed on from generation to generation because of the stories they contain.

In a 30-minute speech, try to include at least two or three stories or illustrations. A story is simply a connected series of events with a beginning, a middle, and an end. Stories can be historical, personal, or hypothetical. Personal stories happened to you, historical stories happened to someone else, and the hypothetical is a story that might have happened but did not. A historical story usually begins with facts that place the story specifically in the past. Here are criteria for effectively using stories or illustrations in a presentation.

> *Use your own personal experience that was meaningful or use one from someone else that really made an impression on you.*

Pick the right story for you. Use your own personal experience that was meaningful or use one from someone else that really made an impression on you. For example, here's a story that occurred during a Boyd family outing.

While attending the 1991 Indianapolis 500 race, we were seated in the front row where most of the action was. On lap 194, Michael Andretti and Rick Mears were dueling for the lead when Mears passed on the right. The crowd gasped. As a result he was able to win the race--his fourth in 14 years of running the Indianapolis 500. After the race, a reporter asked Mears if he remembered the last time he passed on the right. He said, "That was the first time. I simply did what I had to do to win." This story supports the idea to have a passion or goal that we pursue at all costs, and our family is in a special position to relate the example. This combines a personal story with historical facts, providing even greater impact.

Be animated in telling the story. Show emotion with your hands, face, and voice. Gestures help describe your subject. If you are telling us a "little boy" story, show how he looks and how tall he is. Reinforce your story highlights with gestures and move toward the audience when you come to the climax of the story. Let them share in the excitement.

> *A good time to tell a story is after a technical section in your speech.*

Make sure your facial expressions correspond to the feelings you want your audience members to have. If you want them to be surprised, open your eyes wide; if the purpose of your story is to produce anger or outrage, furrow your brow and look furious as you narrate. Remember, if your facial expressions look bored, your audience will feel bored. Facial expressions, such as yawns, are contagious. One story that we like to tell is about the day our granddaughter Kinley was born. She was crying and the new parents were eager to console her. For months before she was born, her dad would "sing to her" every night. New mother Gina said, "Josh, why don't you try singing to her?" And as he softly sang "You are my sunshine, my only sunshine, you make me happy…," the baby stopped crying, listening to her father's familiar voice. Our singing is not the highest quality, but when we sing these lines, the audience never seems to mind. When you tell such personal stories that tug at the heartstrings, you get a strong emotional response that ties the audience in to what you are saying.

Be specific in telling the story. Answer the questions Who? What? When? and Why? For example, don't just say, "Theodore Roosevelt was almost killed by an assassin's bullet." Instead, say, "In the Presidential Campaign of 1912, Teddy Roosevelt was about to deliver a campaign speech in Milwaukee. As he was leaving his hotel, a man leaped from the crowd of supporters and shot him point-blank in the chest. He reeled back as if mortally wounded, but when his aides rushed to him and tore open his shirt, they found only a flesh wound. You see, the bullet had been absorbed by the speech manuscript and eye glass case in his breast pocket." This particular story also gives a great opportunity for acting out the story you are telling.

Have a clear sense of direction in telling the story. Don't get bogged down in details, but instead make sure each detail and description contribute something to the flow of the story. Try to keep the story under two minutes; the longer the story, the more effective it must be. The audience will not be happy if you take five minutes to tell a story that does not relate to the main point. One of the keys to Ernest Hemingway's success as an author was his no-frills, direct approach to storytelling in books such as *A Farewell to Arms*. The same straightforward technique will help emphasize your stories' points. If you are having trouble condensing your story, write the narrative out and analyze each sentence to determine value in making your point.

> *Keep an "Idea Book" to jot down sayings you see or hear and the skeletal facts of your personal experiences.*

Always connect the story with the point you are making. Don't tell a story just because you think it is entertaining. You might use a summary statement like, "The point we learned from the story is…." Tie your story to the conclusion you want your audience to draw, such as, "Roosevelt's experience shows us that the pen can literally be mightier than the sword--or in this case, even the bullet."

A good time to tell a story is after a technical section in your speech when the audience may be getting bored or when your material lacks concrete support. A story is a good way to bring attention back to you, especially if the story is self-deprecatory. At times, Steve tells the audience that he is nervous about being introduced as a professor because he is mindful of the essay a child wrote about Socrates. "Socrates was a famous Greek teacher who went around giving people advice. They poisoned him." As you can see, the story is a means to add the human element, humor, and even suspense to an otherwise technical presentation.

To accumulate a collection of stories, keep track of your own experiences that will interest people. Think of your experiences in terms of topics you cover. Follow the old adage: "Don't think it, ink it." Keep an "Idea Book" where you jot down sayings you see or hear and the skeletal facts of your personal experiences. As you try them out on friends, you will be able to tell if the story is effective in making your point.

You can often find historical stories in nonfiction books that are not familiar to the general populace and that can have marvelous applications to your material. Books that have been helpful to me include *The Perfect Mile* by Neal Bascomb, *Mountains Beyond Mountains* by Tracy Kidder, *Never Have Your Dog Stuffed* by Alan Alda, and *Driving with* the *Devil* by Neal Thompson. Browse *The New York Times Book Review* to keep up with current works.

Talk to older people about their experiences because they sometimes have lived through significant events and have a unique perspective. For example, we had a friend who survived on the Arizona when it was bombed at Pearl Harbor. His take on those events was powerful.

As you accumulate your stories, you will find that some stories fit several different situations and you can use them over and over. They become your own personal stock of stories.

Stories are a highly versatile speaking technique. Learn to use stories to get attention, to support a point, to prompt a feeling, to explain a technical point, or for a dramatic conclusion. The "Once upon a time. . ." approach helps you to be a better speaker by reaching "The End" with more effectiveness and style.

Pay Attention to Delivery

Knowing it is easy; telling about it is the hard part.
~Tom Booker in
Nicholas Evans' The Horse Whisperer

How ideas are presented often determines how much value they seem to offer. Delivery is the source of your contact with the speaker's mind. Thus to deliver your presentation well helps insure that the information you are sharing with the audience will be assimilated and put to use. In all aspects of speaking, delivery plays a significant role, especially with humor. Red Skelton said, "It is not what you say that is funny, it is how you say it." Delivery in speaking involves everything but the words themselves. That includes the use of the voice, hands, facial expression, eyes, posture, and space.

Your voice must demonstrate excitement and energy to avoid a monotone pitch. You can do this by incorporating the *pause and punch*. You *pause* before proper nouns or statistics and then *punch* them out. In addition, you speed up to show excitement and slow down to indicate drama and suspense. As Mark Twain said, "One word may be effective, but no word is as effective as the rightly timed pause."

In a sense, to use your voice effectively, you are putting music in your speech since you are doing the same kinds of things a vocalist may do—speeding up, slowing down, pausing, getting louder or getting softer, and punching out certain words.

As Dr. Catherine Armstrong of Manchester Metropolitan University, UK, says, "If you listen to great orators such as Martin Luther King, it actually takes them a long time to say each sentence....nerves mean that most of us speak too quickly."

Use your hands to describe and reinforce the point you are making. Just imagine the following joke without using your hands.

A man is pulled over to the side of the freeway by a state trooper for speeding. He goes up to the driver's window and sees in the back seat several sharp knives. The trooper says to the man, "I'm going to have to arrest you for possessing those weapons in your back seat."

The man replies, "You don't understand. I'm a juggler for the Barnum and Bailey Circus and the knives are a part of my act. Let me show you." So he gets out of the car by the side of the highway and begins to juggle the knives.

About that time, two guys pass them in the outside lane and one says to the other, "They're really getting tough on those sobriety tests, aren't they!" You have to describe and reinforce with gestures to help people enjoy the joke.

Keep your gestures under control. Adapt the size of your gestures to the size of the room. If you have a big room and high ceilings, use gestures from the shoulder out; if you have a small room with low ceilings, use gestures from the elbow out. Keep your hands away from your face so you won't diffuse the impact of either facial expression or gestures. Instead of pointing to your audience with your gestures, "embrace" them by reaching out with your full hand and bringing them in to you.

Eye contact is vital to your delivery. Eye contact is a visual handshake with your audience members. Without looking directly at members of your audience, you cannot determine if they are listening and understanding your message. Look at small clumps of people in the room and in doing so you will be able to look directly at people within that clump; in a short period of time you can engage all of your audience with your eyes. An ancient proverb states that "the eyes are the window of the soul." This describes how important it is to a speaker to look at the eyes of the audience.

You exemplify your level of self-confidence by your posture and space. Avoid slouching by standing on both feet with your weight equally distributed on the balls of your feet between seven and twelve inches apart. "Plant" your feet to fend off the tendency to pace or bounce. Do not move away from the audience. To emphasize a point, take a step toward the audience. Consequently, if you end up in someone's lap you'll know you had too many points!

> *Eye contact is a visual handshake with your audience members.*

A good example of moving toward your audience was the preacher whose text was Revelation 22:12. As he was speaking, he lost his train of thought so he just kept repeating his text: "Behold, I come quickly!" Each time he said it, he took a step toward his audience. Finally he fell off the stage and onto an elderly lady sitting on the front row.

"Oh, ma'am! I am so sorry!" he said, jumping to his feet.

"Don't apologize to me!" she answered. "You told me three times you were coming!" We don't want to suffer such consequences by too much movement in our speeches.

ATTENTION!

Where you stand is also an important part of using space in your delivery. You want to stand about the same distance from most members of the audience. That way everyone feels equally attended to by the speaker. If the speaker stands to one side or the other from the audience, the audience on the far side may feel left out. Certainly you can move when appropriate throughout the presentation, but you want to have a "center" of the room which is your spot to stand when not moving for a specific purpose. One of the ways of being in the right place as you speak is to center your delivery around the audience, not the lectern or table you are speaking from.

Once you start speaking, the audience's attention can follow you to wherever you are. This may mean moving into the audience on occasion or moving to one side of the room for emphasis. You may move to a different location so the audience
can see your visuals or demonstration better. If you are answering questions you may want to move toward the person asking the question. Or you may want to nonverbally include certain members of your audience with eye contact and embracing gestures as you tell a story. Don't just stand behind or to the side of the lectern as you speak. Let the audience determine where you stand and what gestures and eye contact you incorporate as you deliver your presentation.

Finally, look pleasant as you speak; smile, look expectantly for positive feedback, and change facial expression to match the content of your presentation. Your face is the object of your listeners' attention when you begin to speak, so work to express the feelings behind your content through your expression. Begin with a smile and a pleasant demeanor; that will encourage you to be engaging throughout your presentation.

Although in this chapter you see delivery broken into parts, keep in mind that all of these elements work together to get the ideas from your mind into the minds of the audience. If your nonverbal contradicts what you are saying, the audience will respond first to what they see rather than

> *Delivery is the source of your contact with the speaker's mind.*

what you say in your message. If you mention that you are really excited about your topic yet you have no energy in your voice, your hands are holding on to the lectern tightly, and you have no facial expression to show excitement, then your credibility will suffer. The nonverbal has believability over your words. Make sure when you practice aloud that your delivery agrees with your content.

ATTENTION!

Another way to use nonverbal to more powerfully deliver your material is to adapt your delivery to the audience response. If the audience appears to be lethargic, you may want to speed up your rate of speaking or increase your volume. If the audience seems tense, perhaps you might soften the volume and use smaller gestures, slowing down your rate. If the audience does not seem to be looking at you as you speak, you might point to a visual or gesture with a prop you are using; that will usually motivate them to make eye contact with you again. If, because of puzzled looks on their faces, you feel the audience may not understand the point you are making, you might pause more to give them extra moments to assimilate the information you are giving. If they look too serious, you might smile more or have more pronounced facial expressions; they may respond in kind.

> The nonverbal has believability over your words.

Learn to anticipate where the audience may laugh, or feel emotional, or be ready to ask a question. If you can anticipate well, you can use your delivery to underscore what they are experiencing. When the audience is laughing, you need to pause longer to let them enjoy the experience you have provided for them. For the anticipated question, you may look expectantly at the group. For the emotional impact, you may soften the volume or change the rate of speech to further engage them. To change any of the above intellectual or emotional contexts, you might step in a different direction to let them know you are ready to change moods.

Certainly content is more important than delivery, but you have to keep the attention of the audience to insure that the message will make it into the minds of the listener. Delivery does that. Work on your delivery so that it calls attention to you subject and not to your delivery style itself.

Pay Attention to Persuasion

The best speeches are those in which you tell people things they don't want to hear in order to get them to believe things they don't want to believe, so they'll be motivated to do things they don't want to do.
~Lee Iacocca

One of the hardest tasks for a speaker is to motivate an audience to action. As Charles Garfield stated, "You don't go through life motivating people; you jump start them and you can't jump start anyone unless your own battery is charged."

This is persuasion: to change the beliefs, actions, or behaviors of the audience. Of course since motivation is an "inside job," audience members in reality have to motivate themselves. The job of the persuasive speaker is to create an environment where audience members will want to change their beliefs or actions.

In your speeches, seek to touch both the emotions

and the intellect. The axiom "people buy on emotion and justify with logic" applies here. Not only does the speaker want to give good reasons but also wants the audience to feel emotion about the topic as well. Don't go to the grocery store hungry because if you do you will spend more due to your feeling of hunger; emotion affects action. Eliciting emotion from people in your audience requires the use of stories and description. Along with statistics and other factual or explanatory material, include a story. Stories connect with people at the heart level. If you want to motivate the audience, tell a story about how what you are advocating has affected people's lives.

If you don't have time to tell a story, describe the scene that needs change or the action you wish the audience to take. Whatever your persuasive purpose is, with words you visualize what will happen to make things easier for the listener to take action. Description supplies color to a black and white picture.

You need "WOW" factors in every persuasive message. A "WOW" is any material that makes the listener think "Wow! I did not know that," or "Wow! What a powerful example!" For example, including statistics in a comparison can result in a "WOW." While visiting Niagara Falls, we learned that going over the falls in a barrel is like jumping off a 20-story building at 219 miles per hour. That combination supplies a "WOW" factor. Arrange your message so that every ten minutes there is a "WOW" factor in your content.

A practical way to be persuasive is to tell how what you are advocating works elsewhere. If you want your community organization to raise money for a new city library, find a similar city that is using the same procedure successfully and present that as a case study. We do that on a personal level frequently. We go to a movie or read a certain book because someone else saw the movie or read the book and recommended it to us. We go to a certain location on vacation because a friend went there and had a great experience. As you research information on your topic or issue, find examples of when what you are advocating has worked in other places.

> *You need "WOW" factors in every persuasive message.*

A third way to be persuasive is to use testimony of people your audience respects. For example, Steve speaks a lot on the value of public speaking skills. He is always looking for credible people who testify that public speaking skills helped them become successful. He uses a story from Lee Iacocca's autobiography which credits early public speaking training as a major reason for his leadership ability.

Daniel Webster, one of the great speakers in American history, said, "If all my talents and powers were to be taken from me by some inscrutable Providence, and I had my choice of keeping but one, I would unhesitatingly ask to be allowed to keep the power of speaking, for through it, I would quickly regain the rest." Those kinds of testimonials are very helpful in convincing people to take public speaking training. If you know your audience well, you will have a good idea of whom they respect and thus can cite those authorities to reinforce your ideas.

When possible, use several sources as evidence. Don't rely on one source to support your claims. Incorporating several sources gives depth to your ideas in the minds of your audience. At the least, if you use several sources you have a better chance that one or two of the sources will be accepted by your audience. If you use just one source, audience members may feel you have a strong bias in one area or that you couldn't find other support. Several sources will give the assurance that you have an objective approach to your topic.

As is stressed in Chapter 6, "Pay Attention to Opening and Closing," make clear what you want your audience to do as a result of your presentation.

When Daniel Boone and the young men from Fort Boonesborough were captured by the Shawnee, Chief Blackfish allowed Daniel Boone to make closing arguments as to whether or not the white men should be killed. In his plea, Boone said, "...You have got all the young men. To kill them, as has been suggested, would displease the Great Spirit, and you could not then expect future success in hunting or war. If you spare them, they will make you fine warriors and excellent hunters to kill game for your squaws and children...Spare them, and the Great Spirit will smile upon you." The vote was fifty-nine for death, sixty-one for life. His direct approach saved twenty-eight American lives.

> *When you incorporate several sources it gives depth to your ideas in the minds of your audience.*

Don't supply information overload to make your point. Avoid saying "I want to give you eight reasons why you should accept my proposal." Audiences will lose interest quickly. Instead, limit your reasons to two or three—or four at the most. Don't overwhelm them with too much evidence. Give too much information and the audience won't remember anything, let alone be persuaded.

Keep your best evidence to the end. Remember, people tend to remember best what you say last, as stressed in Chapter 6. Like a good mystery novel, a powerful persuasive presentation should build to a climax. Spend the early part setting the stage and providing good informative material. Keep building your argument so that your strongest reason and evidence comes near the end.

Persuasion also depends on energy the speaker exudes in motivating the audience. You want your excitement to permeate your content through pleasant facial expressions, gestures which describe and reinforce, eyes that connect with the eyes of the audience, and a voice that punches out and speeds up to drive home specific ideas. You can't be persuasive, no matter how powerful the content, if your presentation is delivered in a monotone voice and your hands remain bound to the lectern.

On a Caribbean cruise a woman leans too close to the side of the boat and falls overboard. People hear her screams, and then they see an elderly gentleman jumping over the side. He swims to her and keeps her afloat until a life jacket is thrown to them, saving her life. The ship decides to throw a party for the hero and after they toasted him, he was asked to say a few words. He took the microphone and said, "I have just one question—who pushed me?" We don't want to be "pushy" in our efforts to persuade, but if you choose some of the strategies in this chapter you will be able to influence your audience in positive ways. As Joseph Conrad said, "He who wants to persuade should put his trust not in the right argument, but in the right word. The power of sound has always been greater than the power of sense."

Pay Attention to Credibility

You only have to do a very few things right in your life as long as you don't do too many things wrong.
~Warren Buffett

Often speakers have to deliver presentations with unpleasant content. The vice president must announce a hiring freeze or a downsizing. The human resource director speaks to the employees about a benefits package with fewer benefits. The professor gives discouraging news about a recent test on which the students did poorly. If you are often speaking in difficult situations, developing credibility is key to having your content considered and accepted. Speakers will have little or no impact on audiences if audience members don't respect them and what they have to say.

History provides us a good example of the power of an actual presentation that created credibility. In 1952, Dwight Eisenhower was running for president with Richard Nixon as his vice-presidential candidate. Charges surfaced, however, that Nixon had illegally used some campaign contributions, and

Eisenhower considered dropping Nixon from the ticket. In what became known as the "Checkers Speech," Nixon defended himself in a 30-minute, nationally televised speech. With his wife Pat sitting in the background, he defended his ethics, at one point holding up a piece of paper he claimed was the result of an audit of his books finding him blameless.

Nixon did admit, however, that some supporters had given his children a dog. He said the kids had named the dog "Checkers," and no matter what anyone said, he wasn't going to let them take that dog away. He concluded by asking people to telegraph or mail the Republican National Committee opinions of whether or not he should continue to run with Eisenhower. The overwhelmingly positive response assured his place in the campaign. Who knows how much of American history for the next twenty years was changed because of a little dog and a presentation that convinced people of Richard M. Nixon's credibility!

What makes an audience trust a speaker or believe that he or she is a reliable source? Whom can you trust to have your best interests at heart? Let's look at some practical ways a speaker can maintain and enhance credibility.

First, act in ways consistent with the message of the presentation. This can be as simple as showing concern in your tone of voice and facial expression when talking about an issue that is facing the company. Acting disinterested or unconcerned when presenting bad news can offend your listeners. Showing enthusiasm in delivery by quicker movements, more variety, and a faster rate of speech when reading an exciting climax of a positive presentation can produce the same enthusiasm in your audience.

> *Act in ways consistent with the message of the presentation.*

A student began a persuasive speech by spreading garbage out on a table. She said, "What do all of these pieces of trash have in common? They can all be recycled." She gave a good speech on the need for recycling and how to set up community recycling programs. She finished to a nice round of applause; then she gathered up all of the recyclables from the table—and tossed them into the wastebasket in the corner. She obviously didn't understand the need for speakers to act in ways consistent with their messages in order to maintain credibility.

Good preparation is an ethical requirement as well as a practical one. Your audience gives you time and an opportunity, and audience members deserve to hear your best effort. That only comes through careful preparation, as discussed in Chapter 2. If the audience can tell you didn't prepare for them specifically, they will feel betrayed and won't respond positively to your message. Thus the speaker should start preparing several days or weeks before an important presentation is delivered. It is hard to cram for a speech, and the audience can tell when preparation has not been adequate.

Third, show respect for your audience. Don't insult your audience in any way. Racial slurs and profanity are obviously unethical, but in addition, don't show disrespect for people's gender, backgrounds, positions, appearances, or nationalities. Don't put people down because of their lack of knowledge of a topic; sometimes their lack of information is the very reason you have been asked to speak. Don't embarrass any member of your audience.

As Abigail Adams said, "The best index to a person's character is how he treats people who can't do him any good, and how he treats people who can't fight back." Your audience is at your mercy. Don't play a joke on anyone, even if you do receive that person's permission. Playing a joke on an audience member can backfire; the rest of your group might become fearful of being the target of your next joke, causing them to lose trust in you. Poke fun at yourself instead.

Fourth, base your conclusions in your presentation on clear evidence. Support your assertions with relevant facts, statistics, and testimony. Keep track of your sources and be ready to produce them if an audience member has a question. Don't make assertions you can't support or verify. Perelman and Olbrechts-Tyteca write in their book, *The New Rhetoric: A Treatise on Argumentation*, that whatever support you use should be able to satisfy the "universal audience"--that group of all reasonable, rational people. In your outline, each major point should show a variety of evidence. If that is not the case, then eliminate the point or, if it fits, include the evidence with another point you are making.

> *Respect the time of your audience. Know what time you are expected to finish—and finish at that time.*

Fifth, choose topics that are consistent with your personal beliefs that you live out on a daily basis. You might be able to craft effective speeches advocating views you do not agree with, but you will be much more effective and ethical if you advocate opinions you actually hold. If you advocate a position which is not something you feel completely comfortable with, this will be communicated to your audience by your delivery style. In choosing material for your presentation, one major criterion is how strongly you feel about the point or support. This is an excellent way to eliminate materials when you have more content than time allotted.

Finally, respect the time of your audience. Know what time you are expected to finish—and finish at that time. It is an insult to your audience members and an abuse of your opportunity to speak to keep them thirty, fifteen, or even ten minutes longer than what is expected. In 1841, President William Henry Harrison inaugural address in freezing temperatures lasted for nearly two hours! As a result, Harrison caught cold which went into pneumonia and he died one month later. So he literally talked himself to death, which we do not want to do to ourselves or our audiences.

All of these ethical principles can be condensed to one, a "golden rule" of speaking ethics: *Treat each audience member as you would like to be treated if you were in your audience.*

Pay Attention to the Words You Speak

Words are like planets, each with its own gravitational pull.
~Kenneth Burke

William Norwood Brigance, speech professor, reminded us that "A speech is not an essay on its hind legs." When people write out their speeches as though they are essays, they are rarely successful in communicating to the audience. Some speakers put you to sleep primarily because the words of the speech were in essay form and meant to be read, not spoken. To use the right words in a speech, you must prepare for the ear, not the eye. Words you speak are different from the words you write. Pay attention to words that will resonate with the ear.

Remember that oral style, the term for speaking for the ear, is more informal. So think ideas, not words, as you prepare and practice your speech. If you write the speech word for word, you will obviously be reading to the audience. You may be tempted to memorize your words, which also leads to a boring presentation. Preparing the speech by concentrating on ideas rather than words will encourage you to be more spontaneous as you speak.

Use short sentences when you speak. This is easier on the ears and gives you more opportunity to pause and add emphasis to key words and thoughts. Short sentences give you more control over the nonverbal parts of the presentation. As Earl Nightingale stated, "Keep your sentences short in a speech so you can breathe in the right places." We add that this will also give the audience more time to assimilate each thought.

> *When you use contrasts in speaking, you are tapping into the essence of being human.*

Mark Twain once told of a Missouri farmer who ran five times for the state legislature without winning. It wasn't because he didn't practice his speeches. He practiced his campaign talks every day while milking. He referred to himself as "your humble aspirant." He referred to his audiences as "my enlightened constituents." He talked of "obtaining a mandate" for his "legislative mission." Then one day even his cow balked at his speeches and kicked him in the teeth. With his front teeth knocked out, the farmer could only speak words of one syllable. As a result, he won his next election and kept getting reelected.

Don't be afraid to use contractions. "I can't understand the policy" is more direct and personal than "I cannot understand the policy." Contractions give the speaker more opportunity for directness, a personal trait that is appealing to most listeners.

Use repetition to anchor the ideas in the minds of the listeners. Your audience only has one chance to get the ideas you speak. Unlike receiving a message through the written word, they cannot go back and reread; they cannot use their TiVo to rewind and hear what you just said. Thus repeat your ideas to help your audience remember. Use internal summary, for example: "Now that we have discussed contractions, let us move on to repetition." Preview your main ideas, repeat key points, and summarize at the end.

Make your speech instantly clear. Use language the audience will understand. Listeners don't have dictionaries to find meanings as you speak and ideally they won't be pulling out a BlackBerry or iPhone to look it up. So immediately after speaking an idea, support the thought with an example or illustration. *Illustrate* literally means "to make bright." You do not want President Warren Harding's reputation for lack of clarity. In fact, historian William McAdoo described his speeches as "an army of pompous phrases moving over the landscape in search of an idea."

Clarity is insured when you answer the "W" questions. As Rudyard Kipling wrote,

> "I keep six honest serving men
>
> (They taught me all I knew);
>
> Their names are What and Why and When,
>
> And How and Where and Who."

Another method for being instantly clear is to define the concept, give an example, and then say the idea again. For example, when Steve is talking about serendipity, he might say: "I'm sure we have all experienced serendipity. We have enjoyed the pleasant feeling resulting when good things happen by accident. Recently, I went to pick up my reserved, mid-sized car at the National Rental Car booth in Toronto.

> *To use the right words in a speech, you must prepare for the ear, not the eye.*

The lady said all they had available at that time was a specialty car—the PT Cruiser—or I could wait a few minutes to get the normal midsized car. I had never driven the PT Cruiser and had wondered how they would drive. So I said I'd take it, and the next day I tooled around in a purple PT

Cruiser! I experienced serendipity at the National Rental Car booth."

An additional way to insure clarity and be appealing to the ear is to use contrasts to show differences. They make an audience think, remember, and assimilate more easily. French Cubist painter Fernand Léger addressed contrasts in his paintings, "I organize the opposition between colors, lines, and curves. I set curves against straight lines, patches of color against plastic forms, put colors against subtly nuanced shades of gray."

You are accustomed to contrasts in life. Novels juxtapose the bad with the good. At dinner you have salads and dessert. You are awake and then you are asleep. You are young and become old. So when you use contrasts in speaking, you are tapping into the essence of being human. Think of ways to show contrast in your next presentation. Here are some suggestions. Point up to a problem and then give the solution; show a need and provide ways to fulfill it; use a few well-placed statistics and tell a story to illustrate what the statistics mean.

Jack Welch in speaking at the Tuck Leadership Forum, said, "We have got to now get together and rally behind all the good stuff here. Get rid of the bad. Fix the bad, right the ship, deal with terrorism and get on with it. But every time you think it is the worst of times, go back through history. Go back through sitting in London in 1940 and 1941 and getting bombed every single day, hundreds of thousands of people killed, and homes wiped out. Do you think they would think these would be the worst of times? They wouldn't think it was the worst of times." To help the audience understand, Welch often used contrasts.

In addition, show contrasts in your style of speaking. Use adjectives that describe and then verbs that show action. Mention the negative and then stress the positive. Lincoln's "Gettysburg Address" is a classic of contrasts: "Battlefield...final resting-place," "brave men, living and dead, who struggled here," "us the living...these honored dead."

> *When you use contrasts in speaking, you are tapping into the essence of being human.*

Another way to pay attention to your words is to use comparisons. Compare what you are talking about to something the audience is familiar with. Include alliteration, metaphors, similes, anaphora, and hyperbole. Alliteration involves the repetition of consonant sounds, such as "...not be judged by the color of their skin, but by the content of their character." Similes use *as, like,* or *than* to compare, whereas metaphors indicate that something *is* the thing it's being compared to. For example, "The boss is a fire-spewing dragon on Mondays," a metaphor, is stronger than "The boss acts like a fire-spewing dragon on Mondays," a simile.

Anaphora is the marked repetition of a word or phrase. Winston Churchill's "We shall fight on the beaches, we shall fight in the landing grounds, we shall fight in the fields. We shall never surrender," and Caesar's classic, "I came, I saw, I conquered" are familiar examples of anaphora.

Hyperbole is exaggeration for effect—to make such an unusual picture in your mind that the point will be memorable. Look at Dave Barry's hyperbole: "...a breed of fashion models who are 8 and sometimes 10 feet tall, yet who weigh no more than an abridged dictionary due to the fact that they have virtually none of the bodily features we normally associate with females such as hips and (let's come right out and say it) bosoms. The leading cause of death among fashion models is falling through street grates." Now that's extravagant exaggeration—hyperbole!

The same Indianapolis 500 driver previously mentioned, Rick Mears was once asked what it was like to drive around the two-and-one-half mile oval in Indianapolis at racing speeds. His response was: "It is like driving down your hallway in your home at 240 miles per hour and turning left into your closet." That really had impact and made the danger of racing instantly clear.

Finally, description is a good way to use words well in a speech. Sometimes you don't need an example; all you need to do is describe what you are talking about. I use the hummingbird in talking about potential and will say: "The hummingbird is the tiniest of birds, yet is quite a spectacle with its shiny feathers, colorful collar, and long beak. It flies 60 miles per hour, takes off vertically, and feeds off over a thousand flowers per day." This gives the audience a vivid picture with words of description.

If you can appeal to the ear, you can often avoid the problem of closed eyes and minds. Develop in your speech the words that provide a positive oral quality to help insure the success of your presentation.

Pay Attention to Humor

It is a great thing to have a sense of humor. To go through life with no sense of the humorous and ridiculous is like riding a wagon without springs.
~Henry Ward Beecher

Three elderly gentlemen were sitting together on a train out of London. As the train approached a station, the first one said, "This is Wembley."

The second one said, "No, this is Thursday."

The third one replied, "Me, too! Let's stop and get a drink."

This story is a great way to include humor in emphasizing the importance of speaking plainly and listening carefully. You don't have to be a comedian to use humor in a speech.

To add a new dimension to your next presentation, consider the use of humor. Appropriate humor relaxes an audience and can break down barriers so that the audience is more receptive to your ideas. Humor can bring attention to the point you are making, and humor will help the audience better remember your point. As Virginia Tooper says, "When the mouth is open for laughter, you may be able to shove in a little food for thought."

Some speakers resist using humor because they fear no one else will laugh or smile. That's why an appropriate definition of humor is the *art* of being funny; the goal of the speaker is to choose material that will be enjoyable to the audience, whether they smile, chuckle, or guffaw.

> *When possible, choose humor that comes from your own experiences or those friends have shared.*

A good place to begin is to think of an embarrassing moment that happened to you. Usually there is an element of surprise, incongruity, or a contradiction which can be funny since humor often contains these elements. A recent embarrassing moment may hurt too much for you to see the humor, but think of one that occurred several years ago. By now you might be able to see how the story can be funny to someone else. Remember another definition of humor: "Humor is tragedy separated by time and space."

When Steve played high school basketball, he was the first on the team who was supposed to run through a paper-covered hoop onto the ball floor. As Steve burst through in triumph, he stumbled and slid all the way across the floor. What was mortifying to him was hilarious to everyone else, and now he can tell that story and enjoy laughing with his listeners.

Another value of using the embarrassing moment is that you are poking fun at yourself, not a member of the audience. Don't risk picking on someone in the audience, even if everyone laughs. You never know when a statement can hurt someone's feelings or seem inappropriate to an audience. Audience members may become uneasy, fearing that you will pick on them next.

You are wise to start with humor that is short, such as a one-liner. Certainly give credit to the person who said it, and having another source for the humor takes the pressure off you. You can get experience before going on to more risky aspects of humor. When Steve talks about creativity and getting out of your comfort zone, a line he found that works well is "Orville Wright did not have a pilot's license." The same thing can be true of referring to a sitcom punch line you heard. This gives you a chance to practice setting up humor, but again, since the humor did not come from you, you feel little pressure for people to laugh.

Probably the least risky use of humor is a cartoon. (Be sure to secure permission to use it.) The cartoon is separate from you and if people do not laugh, don't feel responsible. But be sure everyone can actually see the cartoon! After a pause, always read the caption aloud for the benefit of the visually impaired.

We do not recommend using jokes as your first effort at humor. Sometimes jokes can take away from the depth of your content. Also, with the availability of internet sources and email, jokes are passed around a lot and you risk telling a joke many in the audience have heard. On the other hand, A. P. Herbert said, "There is no reason why a joke should not be appreciated more than once. Imagine how little good music there would be if, for example, a conductor refused to play Beethoven's Fifth Symphony on the grounds that his audience might have heard it before."

> *Start with humor that is short, such as a one-liner.*

There are some jokes that we laugh at no matter how often we hear them. Some lines we wish we'd thought of first, such as "If you lend someone $20 and you never see that person again...it was probably worth it." We can still use them when they fit our topics.

If you can adapt the joke to fit your presentation, then a joke might be fine. You can introduce it with a comment such as, "My situation reminded me of a story you may have heard...." and tell the story. By saying "story" and not a "joke," you won't be embarrassed if no one laughs.

When you use humor, show that you are enjoying yourself. Smile, look expectant, speak with enthusiasm. Humor does not work well if delivered timidly. To make that work, make sure the humor is funny to you. If you don't smile or laugh at the cartoon, joke, one-liner, story, pun, anecdote, or top ten list, then you certainly cannot expect an audience to do so. A key to using humor is only to use humor that makes you laugh or smile.

Before using humor in your speech, practice with small groups of people. Do they seem to enjoy the humor? Even if your experimental group does not laugh or smile initially, don't give up on the humor because the problem might be in the way you are delivering the joke or quip. Watch comedians and notice their timing. Listen to the humor channel on XM radio and match your pacing to the style you hear there.

Steve often uses this line in talking about the importance of listening: "We are geared to a talk society. Someone said, 'The only reason we listen is so we can talk next.'" When he first tried that line, people did not smile; but he worked on the timing so that he paused and smiled after "listen" and that seemed to work. He was rushing through the punch line and did not give people time to be prepared for the humorous part. Practice helped him to become comfortable with that humorous comment. Only use humor in a speech after you are comfortable by memorizing and testing the story, joke, or one-liner.

Never use humor that is in poor taste. Don't use profanity or off-color material. Do not insult a nationality, geographical background, or religious affiliation. Avoid making fun of any physical impairment. In other words, do nothing, even in fun, that would insult or hurt someone. A good rule of thumb is *If you're wondering if certain humor might be offensive, do not use it.*

Pace your humor carefully. Watch your audience for feedback. Do not "step on" your humor if people are chuckling or laughing. Pause and let them enjoy themselves. Continue only when the group has experienced the humor and is getting quiet again. One of the challenges a person faces when using humor for the first time is rushing through the material and failing to pause at appropriate places.

> *Never preview by saying, "I'm going to tell you a funny story." Let the audience decide for themselves.*

When possible, choose humor that comes from your own experiences or those friends have shared. You do not have to worry about people having heard the humor before, and you will feel more comfortable telling about what happened to you. Find such experiences by looking for a humorous line or situation.

To stress to parenting groups that the punishment should fit the unacceptable behavior, Lanita likes to tell about their son Josh being part of a group that made fun of a classmate. Since Lanita taught at his elementary school, the punishment Lanita and Steve levied was for Josh to eat lunch with the child three times a week for four weeks. She ends with, "Of course I wasn't sure it was the right punishment when his teacher said, "Making Josh sit with that child is cruel and unusual punishment. You are the meanest mother I know!"

For example, Steve was making a bank deposit at a drive-in window. When he asked to make a second deposit, the teller said solemnly, "I'm sorry, sir, but you'll have to go around the bank and drive through a second time to make a second deposit." They both laughed and Steve may have a line to work into a speech.

If you have small children, listen for something they say that might be funny to an audience as well. Art Linkletter made a great living on the notion that "kids say the darnedest things." Mike Cope, a minister in Abilene, Texas, tells about a child in his congregation who memorized the

Lord's Prayer to say with his parents at home. He ended it by saying, "Please be seated."

Make sure the humor relates to the point you are making. Do not use humor that is simply there to make the audience laugh. The humor should tie in with some aspect of your speech. For example, Steve tells about his experience of getting braces at age 46 and the difficult time he had getting used to the wires and rubber bands in his mouth. After he tells the story, he makes the point that you may have not had the braces problem he had, but we all have challenges in communicating well. We want to look at ways to be more effective in speaking by identifying these challenges and how to overcome them. The audience enjoys the story but also remembers the point that he's making. If you don't tie your humor to your presentation, the audience may like the humor, but will wonder what point you are attempting to make. Or even worse, they may get involved in your story and not even wonder what your point is.

> *Make sure the humor relates to the point you are making.*

Never preview by saying, "I'm going to tell you a funny story." Let the audience decide for themselves. Look pleasant and smile as you launch into your funny line, but if no one smiles or laughs then just move on as though you meant for the piece of humor to be serious. This approach takes the pressure off you.

Remember you are not speaking for laughs as Jay Leno and David Letterman are in their nightly monologues. Your goal is simply to enhance your presentation and be more effective in communicating ideas. Go for it! Use humor in your next speech. Audiences enjoy having fun.

Although President Lincoln was known for his humor, Judge Owen T. Reeves said of him: "I heard Lincoln tell hundreds of anecdotes and stories, but never one that was not told to illustrate or give point to some subject or question that had been the theme of conversation, or that was not suggested by an anecdote or story told by someone else."

Look at humor as a tool in improving your speech in the manner of attention devices, smooth transitions, and solid structure. Remember, "A smile is a curve that straightens out a lot of things."

Pay Attention to Visuals

Research indicates that we retain only
10% of what we hear; 20% of what we see;
65% of what we hear and see....
~Althea DeBrule

Glazed eyes, clicking on Blackberries, text-messaging—all signs of an uninvolved audience. Seeing that a speaker has a PowerPoint presentation made up of charts and statistics or a series of poster board graphs provokes a feeling of doom and a search for distraction before the speaker even begins. But using visuals does not have to be that way. That same speaker with skills in using visuals can captivate the audience, help them to understand, and move them to action when following the techniques discussed in this chapter. These guidelines apply to computer software such as PowerPoint, a dry board, and flip charts, just as to antiquated formats such as an overhead projector.

The visual aid should indubitably enhance the presentation. Ask yourself, "What would this presentation be without this visual?" If the answer is "not very different," then don't use it. Under those circumstances, the visual aid will seem "forced" to the audience and the value lessened. Never use a visual with neutral value; always use visuals that add to the value of the points you are making.

The visual should be easy on the eyes and large enough to be seen by everyone in the room. The best way to insure this is to put the visual where you will be speaking, find the seat furthest away from it, and determine if you can see the item or read the screen from that seat. If you have to ask an audience, "Can you see this?" you are not really prepared for that presentation!

If you are using a typical two feet by three feet piece of poster board or a flip chart, for example, make sure the letters are at least two inches high for easy readability. Using PowerPoint, font size for slides should be no smaller than 24 point Times New Roman or a similar size in other fonts. Headings for slides should be no smaller than 36 point. The "6 by 6" rule is vital: no more than six lines on a page and no more than six words on a line. This approach keeps the visual from looking too "busy" and makes it easier on the eyes of the audience members.

Introduce the visual properly rather than simply thrusting an object or slide at your audience; explain what the visual will do before you unveil it. In introducing the visual, tantalize the audience: "What I have to show you now will demonstrate how the plan works" is a statement that builds anticipation for what you are about to show. The television weather person often does this ("If you look at this next map you will see a storm system moving in from the northeast. . .") in predicting the weather for the next day.

Use good contrast in colors. With a white flip chart page, blue or green marker gives effective contrast. Red makes a good color to underscore key words or ideas. With PowerPoint, a dark blue template or background with shaded yellow lettering looks professional. Be consistent with color contrast. Remember that there may be more light on the screen than on your computer as you organize your PowerPoint slides. Don't use a great variety of colors even though you have the capability to do so. Just because you *can* does not mean that you *should*, especially with computer software.

> *If you have to ask an audience, "Can you see this?" you are not really prepared for that presentation.*

Bullets are better than numbers on a slide, transparency, flip chart, or poster board. Bullets give equal emphasis to all the points while numbers indicate a ranking. Bullets equalize while numbers prioritize. In addition, you can lose track of the numbers as you are talking, and with bullets numbering is irrelevant. Bullets can add attractiveness to the visual and computer software gives many choices.

Don't allow the visual to take your place as the presenter. Visuals are termed "aids" and not "replacements." Be confident enough of the oral presentation itself that if necessary, your presentation can be effective even without visuals; unforeseen circumstances such as lost or malfunctioning equipment or power failure can put your visuals out of commission and leave you on your own. Steve once had an electrical storm shut down the lights and overhead projector with 400 audience members; another time the projector vibrated due to the noise of the heating system, also making visuals impossible to use.

Be careful where you stand in reference to the visual. Don't turn your back to the audience. Step to the side of the screen and point with your hand or a laser pointer as you speak. Do not block the view of the screen from people in your audience. Do not allow the visual to keep you from talking as you develop it; avoid statements like "This slide is pretty much self-explanatory," followed by a period of silence for audience assimilation. If the point is as visually evident as you indicate, people may wonder why you as a presenter are necessary; if the visual is not so easy to understand, they will become embarrassed by their apparent ignorance. Some speakers allow their visuals to be their presentation. Often this results in the speaker losing control of the audience; in addition, if the visuals fail to communicate the message, so does the speaker!

Be comfortable with your visuals. Practice using them as you prepare the presentation. Never assume visual aids will work. Visual aids complicate matters, and if you have not practiced your presentation using the visuals, you will show hesitancy in working with them in the real presentation. Visuals should not call attention to themselves. You should look comfortable as you incorporate them.

> *Bullets equalize while numbers prioritize.*

When the visual is not in use, hide it from the audience. Humans are a curious lot. If we can't understand something at first glance, we tend to keep looking. Your audience may be so distracted that they lose track of what you are saying. To keep a slide from becoming a distraction, click the *B* or *W* on PowerPoint; have a blank cover sheet for the flip chart. An object can be covered with a bag or put behind the desk or podium until you are ready to use it.

Keep your visual aid simple. Limit yourself to one key idea per visual, one graph per slide. Leave lots of space between lines or in the background of a drawing or picture.

Include most explanations in the content of your presentation, not on the visual itself. Make the visual aid attractive to the eye, but not necessarily a work of art. You want people to get the information or explanation, not be distracted by how beautiful, clever, or complex the visual is. Always say more than you show.

Props can also be effective visual aids. A prop is an object you use in your presentation to help illustrate or reinforce a point or to help the audience remember an idea. Audience members weeks or months later often are able to connect the prop with the point of the speech. Here are some suggestions on how to make the best use of a prop. Make sure the prop relates to the content of your speech. Don't be tempted to use a prop simply because it is unusual or unique; the prop should connect the listener to what you are saying. As soon as you reveal the prop, clarify how the prop relates to a point in your speech.

The prop should be handled easily. Concealing the prop before and after its use should be simple and certainly the object should not be seen as dangerous. Years ago Steve quite effectively brandished and fired a cap pistol to illustrate how Teddy Roosevelt was almost assassinated in the 1912 Presidential campaign. That would never work today with our fear of guns in any public place. He stopped even before that, however, when an elderly lady on the front row seemed to think she'd been shot.

Also, avoid objects which are valuable and thus tempting to be stolen as you are talking to people after the speech. Do not increase the complexity of your presentation by having a prop too heavy, too sharp, or too bulky.

The prop should not overshadow the content of the speech or be so shocking or dramatic that the audience gets stuck on the prop. That can happen in a magic show. The illusion is so powerful that the audience cannot mentally go on to the next part of the magician's show.

> *Just because you* can *does not mean that you* should.

The prop should be easily seen by the audience. Accomplishing this may require careful forethought. You may want a small table near the lectern for the display. You may want to move into the audience with the prop. Hold it at the eye level of the audience, not at your eye level. Watch for audience response to the prop to tell if they can see it easily. Look at the audience, not at the prop. Hold the object for the audience to see long enough for them to assimilate the information about the prop and understand the application.

Conceal the prop before and after its use. People are curious, and if they see it on your lectern or table before you get to that part of your speech, they will be wondering what it is and how it will fit into your speech. Keep the prop hidden behind the lectern or concealed in a box behind the stage curtain. Then when you show it, the audience will give you complete attention.

Prepare the audience for your use of the prop. If it is introduced suddenly and without warning the audience may be so distracted by the surprise that they may lose track of the point you are making with the prop. Even a simple sentence like, "Let me show you an object that will help make my point" will pave the way for the prop.

> *Conceal the prop before and after its use.*

In "High Bid," Steve's keynote speech on communication, he talks about how the tiny hummingbird accomplishes great things considering its size. After mentioning the amazing hummingbird abilities described in Chapter 11, "Words You Speak," to reinforce the point he auctions off an antique roof slate decorated with hand-painted hummingbirds. (The money for the purchase of the painting by the high bidder goes to his or her favorite charity.) We have a lot of fun during the auction with the painting in plain view. The audience gets a chance to connect reaching one's potential with the example of the accomplishments of the hummingbird. This prop is a highlight of the speech and a reminder to the audience of the potential within each of us.

Paying attention to using visuals effectively will encourage your listeners to pay attention to you. Follow the suggestions in this chapter to make visuals an integral addition to your presentation.

Pay Attention to the Handout

If you're going to make a speech, make sure everyone in the room walks away with something to share and remind them of you.
If you don't, you've waste your time.
~Andy Semovitz

The handout reinforces or explains a point you are discussing, whether it is a program outline, pictures, financial summaries, drawings, diagrams, formulas, or a proposal. How to use handouts most effectively seems to be a challenge for many. Ideally, to avoid any distractions during the content of the presentation, the handout would be provided at the end of the program, but that is not always practical. The obvious problem with any handout is that audience members will start reading the handout rather than listening to you speak.

Plan ahead for how you will actually put the handouts in the hands of audience members. If the group is large, you may want to place the material on each seat before the participants arrive. A concern here might be that the person may feel the handout is enough and leave without hearing the proposal or speaker. Also, the person may become engrossed in the handout and not give you optimum attention at the beginning of your presentation. Passing out material to a large number during the presentation, however, may be too awkward and time-consuming. If you decide to pass the materials out during the program, it's a good idea to count how many chairs are in a row or how many chairs are around each table and collate the papers by those numbers. Have assistants from the audience or your company already primed to pass them out at your signal. If you have a small group of four or five this is not a concern.

As you are making the materials available to audience members, do not cover critical information in your presentation. The audience will be distracted while passing sheets down the row or around the table and will begin getting acquainted with the outline, thus missing most of what you say during that time. Keep speaking but include illustrative or auxiliary information so the group will not miss a key point in your presentation. This would be a good time to tell a story or add a personal note about your company or organization. The most effective way is to distribute the handouts on a need-to-know basis. You may want to pass out some documents in parts as you work through the material in the program. This technique will keep the participants from jumping ahead; this takes more time, however, and can sometimes disrupt the pacing of your program.

Once Lanita accidentally printed the back of one page in a packet upside down. Though this was embarrassing to her, everyone seemed entertained by the oddity and paid better attention by turning that page upside down to follow the information.

Provide specific instructions to the audience on how to view the handout before you make the materials available. For example, you can tell them to go to page three at the blue mark and possibly even give a reason. That will keep them from browsing through pages one or two. The more specific you are with directions, the quicker the participants will do what you want them to do. An audience is cooperative if they know what you expect of them. If you finish the handout before you finish your speech, tell them to put the material aside.

> *Provide specific instructions to the audience on how to view the handout before you make the materials available.*

Your handout should be easily explained. If the paper includes words not quickly grasped or an elaborate explanation of the material, you should give them this information in another medium, not as a handout during a presentation. Your handout should be useful information that is immediately pertinent in the minds of the listeners.

Arrange your handout so that audience members will follow your presentation and the handout simultaneously. One way to accomplish that is to leave blanks in the material for them to fill in. This is especially important if you are providing financial data or statistical information. Let the audience fill in the amounts. Having the blanks will make them curious and interested in gaining the information to write in the blank. Another way is to include phrases or key words so that the audience members will want to take notes on the broader explanation you provide orally. Number the pages clearly for easy reference so listeners will quickly go to the place in the material you are discussing.

If you use a similar handout in various situations and possibly year after year, be sure the material is up-to-date. Steve more than once sent in new material for a regular client to copy, but when he got there they had printed the outline on an old template that was out-dated. A way to avoid this is to ask that they send you the printed copy for your approval before they print multiples. Knowing you will see it first will also make them more careful in making copies.

Don't let the handout dominate your presentation. Include visuals or slides that will require the listener to look up at you or the screen. Use words or phrases in your presentation such as "See," "Look with me at...," or "Notice on the screen...." These previews will get audience members out of the handout and back to you, the speaker.

During your preparation, have someone else proofread the handout to insure no grammatical errors or misspellings. Errors in the content can distract the reader and negatively affect your credibility. This should go without saying, but we often overlook errors when we are very familiar with our material.

> *Your handout should be useful information that is immediately pertinent in the minds of the listeners.*

Handouts add complexity and time to your program. The material should contribute to your objectives. If this is not the case, then omit the handout. If you are using a handout in order for the listener to take with them your name, phone number, or e-mail address, either include content that will add to the presentation or simply give them a card containing your contact information. A book list or resource page at the end of the handout will usually insure the value of the handout to the audience.

Handouts best given out at the end of your speech are background notes, the PowerPoint presentation print-out, bibliography, webliography, brief bios of trainers and speakers, list of participants, useful articles, and examples of documentation covered by the presentation.

Keeping the attention and interest of the audience is hard enough when there is no handout to distract them. If you incorporate these suggestions, your handout can be an effective way for your audience to take you with them and to remember the key parts of your program.

Pay Attention to Ceremonial Speeches

***Creativity is piercing the mundane
to find the marvelous.***
~Bill Moyers

At Lanita's brother's wedding, the matron of honor was exceptionally attractive. The best man was single. The bride's name was Nancy and the matron of honor's name was Eileen. When it came time to toast Larry and Nancy, the best man was quite eloquent until he ended by congratulating the happy couple with, "We toast you, Larry and Eileen." This brought hysterical laughter from everyone, and the best man never lived that embarrassing moment down. Incidentally, 30 years later, he is still single!

Toasts, speeches of welcome and introduction, and eulogies are often given by people with little speaking experience. The guidelines here will help you to feel comfortable in carrying out your responsibilities with poise.

The toast is the perfect way to top off the celebration at a holiday banquet, reception, party, retirement dinner, or anniversary. If you have the opportunity to offer a toast, here are some suggestions to avoid the experience of that mortified best man.

The word "toast" originated with the Romans, who browned their coarse bread in a fire. When the bread became too hard to chew, they soaked it in wine. The meaning of "toast" expanded to include the drink in which the bread had been soaked and then the words for the person in whose honor the drink was consumed. The toast is an affirmation of a person or event with words.

To effectively toast the honoree, offer the toast early in the celebration so that no one has had too much to drink. Make sure everyone has an appropriate glass and liquid to participate in the toast and someone close by with whom to clink glasses together at the appropriate moment.

> *Toasts, speeches of welcome and introduction, and eulogies are often given by people with little speaking experience.*

Begin with "I propose a toast." Give the occasion for the toast, why the toast is appropriate for the celebration and your connection to the recipient of the toast. The body of the toast is putting in words how you feel about the person, the event, or the time of the year. Be brief, concise, and direct. Two minutes is the maximum for a toast.

ATTENTION!

The toast is one of the few times when a manuscript is in order. At the least, plan ahead. Do not do an impromptu toast! Avoid this introduction even if it is true: "I didn't really have time to prepare anything, but I want to say...." (The audience will discover it soon enough, or not at all!) Print your words on a note card. Hold the card(s) in your left hand, so that when the time comes you can raise your glass with the right hand to touch glasses with a companion as you conclude the toast. Your last words are the object of the toast.

One of the most disastrous toasts we ever witnessed was from a manuscript, but that was not adequate help for this particular person. She started with events she and the bride had shared in childhood and since; she sobbed hysterically, blew her nose, and apologized again and again. The toast reminded us of the comment, "I spent ten years there one day." The ten minutes she spoke seemed like hours to the uncomfortable guests and probably even more so to the bride and groom.

We sometimes like to include a quotation within the toast. If you are toasting people you might include the anonymous "May you live as long as you want and may you never want as long as you live."

Create a dramatic flourish as you end. You want people to know when you are finished. "Let's all raise our glasses to ...", then *clink* with a partner, and take a sip. There is not a better way of affirming a person and showing appreciation than an appropriate toast.

The most common of all special speeches is the speech of introduction. Often this special speech is too long, too laudatory, and filled with too many clichés. To make a presentation sparkle from the outset, here are some tips on introducing the speaker.

Keep the introduction short. Again, your maximum is two minutes or less, depending on how well the speaker is known to the audience. The primary purpose of your introduction is to qualify the speaker as an expert on the topic to be discussed. If the person is already accepted as an expert, the introduction can be less than a minute.

> *At all costs, avoid saying: "I didn't really have time to prepare anything, but I want to say...."*

Chauncey Depew was a United State Senator around the turn of the century, and his infamous introduction of President William Howard Taft is a classic. He took 45 minutes to introduce the President. (He obviously did not know the "how well known the speaker is to the audience" part!) He finished his introduction by saying, "Now here is a man pregnant with power, pregnant with possibility, pregnant with the great career he has developed. Here is President William Howard Taft!"

Taft, weighing over 300 pounds, stood and patted his expansive stomach. He said, "If it is a girl, I'm going to name it Martha Washington Taft. If it is a boy, I'm going to name it Abraham Lincoln Taft. But if it is gas, as I suspect it is, I'm going to call it Chauncey Depew!"

Another caution is to avoid platitudes: "This speaker needs no introduction...," or "Without further ado...," If the speaker needs no introduction, then why have an introducer? And why introduce "further ado?" Use language that describes what is actually going to happen. "Our speaker will explain...," or "Today's speaker will talk about...." Never say the speaker is the greatest or the best; superlatives about a speaker that are stated before the audience can make its own judgment cause resistance from audience members who want to make up their own minds; such statements also put unnecessary pressure on the speaker. Base what you say on facts: "Our speaker is in much demand. He speaks all over the country each year on this topic."

Here is a basic outline for an introduction.

- **Subject:** Begin by telling the audience what topic the speaker will address. "Tonight we are going learn how to overcome stage fright."

- **Significance:** Emphasize why the audience should listen. "We have all experienced butterflies in the stomach. Our speaker is going to give us techniques on how to control our anxieties while speaking—to make those butterflies fly in formation!"

- **Speaker:** Tell about the speaker. You want to qualify the speaker on the topic and prepare the audience to want to hear what's coming. Choose facts that will make the audience want to listen.

> *If the speaker "needs no introduction," then why are you giving an introduction?*

In addition, to avoid embarrassment and distractions to the audience, check for unfamiliar pronunciation of the speaker's name or other proper nouns associated with him or her. Say the person's name aloud a few times so you are comfortable speaking it. Bring the speaker to the audience in a positive manner. Mention the speaker's name last. Say the name clearly, and begin the applause when you finish. Use a statement like, "Please join me in welcoming Chris Davis." You start the applause to lead an enthusiastic welcome to the speaker. If you follow this model, you will help insure the success of the speaker and create a positive impression of yourself as well.

Often a person giving a thank-you speech has had very little speaking experience. Harrison Ford, in accepting a Golden Globe Award, both gave advice and set the standard for everyone. He said: "Knowing how tight time can be on an awards show, I prepared two speeches, a short one and a long one. I guess I'll give the short one: Thank you. Ah, it appears I have time for the long one, too: Thank you very much."

At conferences, conventions, and all-day meetings, another special speech is the speech to welcome participants and guests. This helps get the meeting off to a good start. Usually this is done by a member of the sponsoring group or a respected leader who represents the body as a whole.

First, mention whom you represent and why they are attending this conference. For example, say, "On behalf of the National Woodcutters Association I am delighted to welcome you to the Axe-Sharpening Conference. You will be glad you are here because you will receive cutting-edge material in the technology of metal-grinding."

Second, predict pleasant experiences for the participants. You might say, "You will benefit from the educational sessions and also the camaraderie of being with people from throughout the country who do what you do. In addition, you will enjoy the special regional foods in the Hansel and Gretel area. We will have a special trip to the Dark Woods on Tuesday as well as free time for your own explorations."

Third, give a brief orientation to the schedule. Any new environment makes a person feel a little uncertain and uncomfortable. One of your responsibilities is to make people feel at ease. Your welcoming speech should help them feel more comfortable with being away from valuable time at work. Thus you might hit the highlights of the conference and perhaps refer to the appropriate pages in their packet.

> *Two minutes is your limit for toasts and speeches of introduction.*

Finally, challenge them to make this the best conference ever. "I know you will make valuable contacts with new resources. You will learn techniques at this conference that you can take home and use immediately to help make your job easier. Thus I challenge you to make note of one idea per session and share those ideas with people here and certainly with associates when you get home." Your last line should be, "We welcome you! Have a great week!"

When you have included these specific elements you have completed the speech of welcome; anything else and you may be taking information from another person who may be speaking at the opening session.

The last ceremonial speech we will consider is the eulogy. "Sometimes when one person is missing, the whole world seems depopulated." This quotation by La Martine could be the beginning of a eulogy, probably the most difficult of special presentations. Because of typically being delivered soon after someone close to you died, the eulogy as a ceremonial presentation usually involves strong emotions.

Funerals today often include non-clergy speakers, so you might be called upon to deliver a eulogy even if you are not a minister. Two recent funerals we have attended, in fact, have included several five-minute eulogies by friends of the deceased in addition to the funeral sermon. This special speaking situation requires that you know your particular role, can be upbeat and not overly emotional, and can keep it short.

First, be sure you know your part in the service. Whom do you follow and what is expected of you? Are you the designated person to represent the company, neighborhood, or family, or are you one of several friends of the deceased who will speak? Keep your remarks related to the position you are expected to fill.

Recently Steve witnessed a woman called on to deliver a eulogy because she was a research associate of the deceased. In keeping with her role, she spoke of the deceased's love of research and how her connection to the deceased revolved around that shared work.

Second, be upbeat. Emphasize things that will comfort the family and friends and leave people in the audience with positive memories. Perhaps the person had a great sense of humor, or showed tremendous compassion, or was devoted to her family, or remembered birthdays. Pick out a couple of these positive traits and then give personal examples illustrating these traits. One of the finest poems for a funeral is "What is Death?" written by Canon Scott Holland in 1919, easily located through Google.

> Funerals today often include non-clergy speakers, so you might be called upon to deliver a eulogy.

Third, keep your remarks short. Generally, you should speak no longer than five minutes. Two or three traits with concise personal examples will fit this time frame. Unless you are the minister, there will usually be other speakers besides you, and a funeral, out of respect for the family members, should not be too long.

Fourth, choose examples that will not make you too emotionally overwhelmed in remembering the deceased. In fact, practice your examples before the service so that you can control your emotions enough to maintain your composure when you are actually in front of the group. Although there is nothing wrong with tears at a funeral, your emotions may overwhelm you unexpectedly and cause challenges if you have not chosen carefully and practiced.

Finally, conclude your eulogy with a line that encapsulates the life of the person you are remembering. This line might be a quotation from one of the person's favorite writers, a line from a favorite hymn or the Bible, or simply something you heard the person say once that you think represents how the deceased would want to be remembered.

We will long remember the ending of President Reagan's eulogy for the crew of the Challenger: "The crew of the space shuttle Challenger honored us by the manner in which they lived their lives. We will never forget them, nor the last time we saw them, this morning, as they prepared for their journey, and waved good-bye, and 'slipped the surly bonds of earth' to 'touch the face of God.'"

Especially if you are known to be a competent speaker, you are likely to someday be called upon to deliver a eulogy. By using this brief formula, you can honor the deceased in a way that will remind everyone of why that person was special.

Pay Attention to Special Situations

***Only when the tide goes out do you discover
who's been swimming naked.***
~Warren Buffett

Speaking is even more challenging and exciting when dealing with the unusual or unexpected. Some situations which go beyond the typical speech involve having technical difficulties, being called on to give an impromptu speech, giving a group presentation, speaking to international audiences for whom English is not the native language, and interruptions from various sources. Here are some suggestions on how to handle the unexpected.

One special situation is when you have an equipment snafu. The lights go off, the public address system goes on the blink, or the room temperature soars or plummets. You can ask your contact person, perhaps the program chair, to find someone to correct the situation. A preventive measure is in advance to get the technology specialist's phone number in case of any technological problem. Often ignoring the situation is best if it's possible for you to continue. If the lights go out and you can continue to speak and keep people calm, you will be the delight of your program chair!

Recently various members of Steve's audience thought they needed to offer assistance in areas he was willing to ignore. Two gentlemen fiddled with the speaker system. Some servers decided to clear a table at the front of the room. When Steve touched "B" to blank his PowerPoint screen, a kind woman thought his projector had failed and went up to try to fix it. Later when he was telling about the situation, he said, "I've never been at a church service where this many people came forward!" If it happens again, he may actually say that to the audience.

All of us at some point have had to speak unexpectedly, either on our own volition or because someone thinks we have something to contribute. This speaking without preparation is known as *impromptu* speaking. You may be at a city meeting concerning zoning laws and have no intention of saying anything, but your strong opinions on the issue prompt you to raise your hand to speak. Or you are called upon by your manager at a staff meeting to report on a project you are involved in and had no forewarning that you were going to be asked to say a few words. How can you handle these situations with poise and competence? You do not want your words to be "full of sound and fury, signifying nothing." Here is a formula that will make you look good and sound on top of things.

Don't hesitate. Act as though you are delighted to have this opportunity to speak. Avoid hemming and hawing and mumbling "I'm not sure what to say," or "I had not given this any thought." Start confidently by making an assertion. For example, if you want to give your thoughts on recycling, you might begin, "I believe we should have bi-weekly pick-up to show we are serious about recycling." Then give evidence that would illustrate your point. This is where you include your personal experience with the matter. You might have lived in another community where recycling was started and you can give a case study of the success you had in that town.

> *If the lights go out and you can continue to speak and keep people calm, you will be the delight of your program chair!*

Once you have given your minute to a minute-and-a-half response, end by repeating the opening assertion. This is a neat little package that allows you to make a point in an organized and easy to understand structure.

Don't speak more than a couple of minutes. Speaking for several minutes may mean you run out of new material, stray from this organization pattern, or even say things that are not logical, relevant, or insightful.

You can't really prepare for an impromptu speech, but before any sort of gathering of people, you can consider what topics will be discussed and how they might relate to you. Thinking ahead will allow you at least to consider areas where you might have input so that you are not blindsided by a question or request from a peer or the leader of the event.

Certainly a prepared speech will have more impact, but a poised and confident delivery coupled with a concisely organized point and support will enhance your credibility. You will be seen as someone others can depend on always to speak with insight, clarity, and conciseness.

More and more, our audiences include people from other countries. How do we adapt to audiences of people who may not be familiar with our culture? Here are some speaking tips for these kinds of situations.

If you are speaking to an audience which requires a translator, the first change you must make is to cut the length of your speech in half. The translator will need equal time to speak your words in the language of the audience and may take even longer than you. He or she needs time to assimilate what you have said and express those ideas in another language.

An effective way to connect with an international audience in the beginning is by giving a greeting in a language represented in the audience. If you had several Portuguese speaking members of your audience, you might begin with "ola," as a way of saying "hello" to the audience.

Even assuming your audience can understand your native language, here are important considerations. Speak more slowly than usual. When communicating in a second language, the listener needs more time to assimilate and

> *Careful articulation is crucial with international audiences.*

understand. Make yourself pause at the ends of sentences and ends of thoughts to help you pace the rate of speech, giving the audience members longer to comprehend what you are saying. If you speak rapidly, not only will the audience members not be able to assimilate quickly enough, but the lack of pauses makes the words hard to distinguish clearly.

While talking to a Ukrainian, our son Josh asked, "What did you do this week-end?" The person to whom he asked the question immediately picked up his dictionary and began thumbing through the pages. Josh asked him what he was looking for and his response was "whadja."

Articulate your words carefully. We often become lazy with our speech habits and don't use tongues, lips, and teeth to clearly articulate our words. Words run together. Look for the furrowed brow or the quizzical look that remind you to articulate more carefully and pause more frequently. Other examples are "where'd ja," "come-ere," and "lotsa." Our normal blending of words can make understanding difficult, so be helpful to ESL (English as a Second Language) listeners by avoiding contractions when possible. Saying "did not" rather than "didn't" also slows your pace, thus enhancing understanding.

Occasionally you can use a particular word in their language. For example, in talking about "a little bit," if you had Italians in your audience you could say, "Or as you would say in Italian, 'umpo.'" If there were Thai people in your audience, you might say, "Our children like to play 'peek-a-boo,' or as you would say in Thai, 'som-o.'" That reference to a word in their language gives them a mental break as well as providing more time to think about what you are saying. They also appreciate your effort to relate to them.

Rarely tell jokes. Many jokes are culture-specific and would not have a clear meaning to the international part of the audience. Beginning a joke with "Two good ole boys were driving down the interstate..." would not be clear to people who did not understand the phrase "good ole boys" or our interstate highway system. Some punch lines might have different meanings when taken literally by those for whom English is a second language.

When possible, give more than one meaning or explanation of a word or phrase. If the person hears multiple explanations, he or she will be more likely to figure out the meaning of your thought. To explain snow plow, you could begin by saying it removes snow from the road quickly and efficiently and end with "the snow plow is usually a metal scraper at the front of a truck."

> *Don't tell jokes to an international audience since most jokes are culture-specific.*

Avoid the use of idioms and figures of speech. The idiom is a phrase where the words together have a different meaning from the individual words. An example would be "I'm going to give it a lick and a promise." A figure of speech might be "...looked like something the cat dragged in." These kinds of expressions only confuse the international audience. If you are accustomed to using colorful figures of speech, you will need to revamp your approach for your international listeners.

Use gestures to emphasize what you are talking about. If you are explaining a way to operate a piece of farm machinery, you might show with a gesture shifting gears, or working the hydraulic lift, or shutting off the engine. In giving directions, demonstrate with gestures the specific instructions. Put a large emphasis on the nonverbal to complement the verbal.

Don't be anxious when you know you have ESL people in your audience. If you use the suggestions discussed here, you will be a big hit (*not* a huge blow to the head!) with the group.

Another challenging situation is when you find out you need several people to provide the expertise the client or program chair seeks and thus a group is formed to deliver one speech. Handling the group presentation with coordinating themes and strong support or evidence plus integrating three or more different personalities and approaches into one 45-minute presentation is not easy. Here are some suggestions on how to make the group or multi-person presentation effective.

First, appoint one of the speakers to be in charge. If this does not happen, no one will take responsibility when the unexpected occurs, and the group will lose credibility. In addition, when a question is asked, the speaker in charge immediately defers to the person with the appropriate expertise, eliminating any uncertain pause because no one knows who will answer the question.

Second, each speaker should know what each of the other speakers is going to say. This knowledge will help each person avoid duplication of material and each can make appropriate references to another speaker's content if it applies, insuring continuity among the different speakers.

Third, the last words of each speaker should segue into what the next speaker will cover. This adds unity to the entire presentation and gives the new speaker a smooth opening to his or her material. An example might be, "Now Susan will cover the financial aspects of our proposal and help you understand the benefits this will give you."

> *A rehearsal is a necessity for a group presentation to go well.*

Fourth, if possible, the strongest speaker should end the group presentation. As we discussed in Chapter 6, "Pay Attention to Opening and Closing," the ending is the most important part of the presentation; people remember best what you say last. You want to have an ending speaker who can show passion and enthusiasm for the topic discussed.

Finally, a rehearsal is essential. The group members need to get a feel of the complete message to see how they can best contribute. In addition, with several people speaking, the amount of time each speaker will take is crucial. This rehearsal allows the group to time the presentation and to make adjustments in each portion in order to be under the time limit; the more people involved the more unpredictable will be the total time. With everyone being able to hear each other, the feedback of each contributing speaker will improve the quality of the whole presentation. Extraneous material can be eliminated as well.

Following these suggestions will contribute to an excellent group effort. The audience will see the presentation as a unified whole, not a series of different presentations.

Probably the most difficult unexpected situation for a speaker is when there are interruptions during the speech. Once, in the middle of Jay Leno's monologue, a cell phone rang in the audience. He walked into the crowd and on national television said, "Here, let me talk to your friend."

He answered the woman's phone, saying, "This is Jay Leno. I'm in the middle of my monologue right now, so is there a message I can take?"

This kind of situation may be where the term "thinking on his feet" originated. The extreme is heckling, when someone is shouting to be heard above the speaker. This is rare, but other interruptions are not. Audience members talking among themselves, someone snoring, cell phones ringing, people walking out of the room, hallway noise, and servers coming in the room to pick up dishes are all common interruptions.

When this happens, you should first ignore the action or the sound. Often an interruption works itself out without the speaker doing anything. The phone will be turned off or answered outside the room, people will quit talking among themselves, someone will awaken the snorer, and the hallway noise will pass. If this does not happen, as a last resort you can address the issue. If someone is responding aloud about something he disagrees with, you might say, "If you will allow me to finish my presentation I will allow you to respond

> *Often peer pressure will take care of distractions and interruptions.*

during the question and answer period." To the person obtrusively clearing dishes, saying, "I'll be through in 10 minutes and then you can clear the room of dishes," can solve the problem. If you ignore the distraction, peer pressure will be likely to take care of the situation. Often a person at the table with talkers will "shush" them or someone in the audience will ask the server to leave the room until the speech is over.

Whatever the situation, do not panic and don't give in to the unexpected. Let your actions show that you remain in charge even though you may not be able to continue your speech until the situation is alleviated. With the exception of the group presentation, these situations must be dealt with as you are in front of the audience; with the group presentation the challenge is anticipating the unpredictable when several people are delivering a speech together. If you follow the suggestions in this chapter, your speech content will be enhanced and your credibility will increase because of the professional way in which you handled the difficult situation.

Pay Attention to Common Sense in Speaking

Common sense and a sense of humor are
the same thing,
moving at different speeds.
A sense of humor is just common sense, dancing.
~William James

Everyone does dumb things at times. For speakers this can be a challenge because you may have an audience of 100 who see and hear you act foolishly. This chapter is about common sense techniques to avoid embarrassing yourself in front of an audience. You don't want said of you Benjamin Franklin's comment: "Here comes the orator, with his flood of words, and his drop of reason!"

Always be concerned about time. Be present early for your speaking engagement. The person in charge will be relieved to see the speaker early. Audience members who see you present early will be impressed. Don't go overtime with your presentation. If you are to speak 30 minutes, never speak 35 minutes. In fact, stop at 28 minutes. Show respect for the time of the listeners. If the previous speaker went overtime, cut some of your material to help the meeting to stay on schedule. The planners will be grateful for your professionalism.

Pronounce proper nouns correctly. Check ahead of time to make certain you know how to pronounce the name of the organization you are speaking to, key names of people in the group you will be conversing with, and any buzz words the audience may have in common. If you are speaking in a strange town check out the pronunciation based on how the people who live there pronounce the city. For instance Lafayette, Tennessee, is Luh FAY ette and Lafayette, Indiana, is Lah fay ETTE.

Audiences are more intelligent and more demanding than ever before. Thus find out before you speak the knowledge level of the group on your topic. You don't want to define or explain terms that the audience already knows, but neither should you skip over definitions of unfamiliar words. Determine who the experts are in the room and perhaps use them as a resource at times.

Be pleasant but not pushy in the way you interact with the audience members before and after you speak. Don't be demanding if the room is not set up the way you want or the public address system is not quite as you prefer. Be willing to go with the flow and adapt the best you can. In talking to individuals before and after the presentation, be a good listener by asking open-ended questions that engage the other person. Don't reinforce the stereotype that all speakers want to do is talk.

Be sincere and pleasant as you relate to the audience members whether a large audience or a casual conversation one-on-one. We have a friend who is often not invited to lunch with a group because they know she will dominate the conversation and no one else will get a chance to talk. A good way to monitor yourself is always to ask a follow-up question to whatever the person says. Many people make themselves unwelcome in conversations because they constantly come back with, "That reminds me of when I…" or "…when my daughter," or "…when my son." Follow the other person's thoughts extensively before inserting your own.

> *Audiences are more intelligent and more demanding than ever before.*

Another way to pay attention to common sense is to play to your strengths as a speaker. In a recent public speaking assignment, the students had to use exaggerated gestures and body movement to describe how to do something, such as eating a piece of pizza or changing a tire. One of the students in the class is a quadriplegic. Steve was uncertain as to how the student would handle the assignment. The young man responded in a marvelous way by showing how he taught his niece to wiggle her ears! He gave a lively demonstration from the neck up. The audience loved his presentation and he did an outstanding job. He demonstrated a powerful principle in speaking: play to your strengths.

In attempting to improve our speaking, we often concentrate on overcoming our weaknesses. On a video playback of a presentation, we look for all our mistakes and formulate ways to improve. There is nothing wrong with doing that—if you also will evaluate what your strengths are and work to accentuate your strong points as a speaker.

For example, if you tell stories well, be sure to include stories in your speeches. If people often laugh at your comical remarks, include humor whenever appropriate. If you have a naturally lively delivery style, don't stand behind a lectern when you speak; stand to the side or in front of the lectern so you can optimize your own delivery style. If you have an uncanny ability to elicit audience participation, then allow time for that in any speech you deliver. Conversely, if you do not know how to use PowerPoint, then don't.

We remember great speakers for the strengths they possessed. Abraham Lincoln told great stories. He was a voracious reader and had a variety of life experiences from which to draw material for his speeches.

President John Kennedy was a master of oral style. He had a knack for assembling great minds to help write his speeches and worked with them in determining just the right word in important presentations.

President Ronald Reagan used humor in his presentations to draw an audience to him. His acting background no doubt aided him in including humorous lines in his speaking. Think about past life experiences which might help you determine your strengths and hone in on those effective traits that can be incorporated in your presentations.

The common sense conclusion: if you play to your strengths you will eventually weed out the weaknesses by not dwelling on them. Instead, squeeze them out of your presentation by relying on your strengths. We see this philosophy in team sports. The coach or manager will put the player in the game or contest where he or she can best incorporate strengths. This has led to very specialized positions, from the middle reliever and closer in baseball to the shooting guard in basketball.

Another approach to enhance your strengths as a speaker is to choose audiences which respond best to your style of delivery, to your content, and to the type of speech you present. This may not always be possible, but after you have delivered a lot of speeches you will know which audiences respond best to your speaking. For example, you may not seem to connect well with those who deal with finances, but you seem to be generally successful with sales people. Or perhaps your audiences respond best when you deliver a speech which helps them understand new or difficult concepts and maybe not as well if you are seeking to move them to action.

> *If you play to your strengths you will eventually weed out the weaknesses by not dwelling on them.*

Don't make a member of the audience look bad. If a person asks a question that is about something you covered carefully in the speech, be tactful in reviewing what you have already said. If a person misunderstands what you think is a simple point, don't call attention to that but rather give another example to make the point clear. If a question seems out of place, you might mention kindly that the question is not related to the topic being discussed, but that you will be glad to discuss it with the person after the speech.

Be sensitive to the themes that the person or audience may feel very strongly about and don't make light of them. If you are speaking in Indiana, for example, you'd do best to avoid taking sides between the Indiana Hoosiers and the

Purdue Boilermakers. Whereas each nickname is ripe for derision, wisdom dictates that you avoid jokes about either. If there's an unusual statue in the middle of the town square, don't belittle it. As in the case of the Boll Weevil Statue in Enterprise, Alabama, local citizens may be proud of their monument, even if it honors an agricultural pest. Learn the loyalties and allegiances that a group of people has and respond to them with grace, leaving out negative references.

Finally, don't make excuses for your inadequacies. Don't tell an audience that you did not have time to prepare; they will figure that out soon enough. Don't apologize for a weak voice or bad cold that the audience might not even notice if you don't mention it.

Common sense can come through learning from your own mistakes or those of others. If you take the advice in this chapter, you can avoid looking foolish and respond with common sense and sensibility.

Pay Attention to Questions and Answers

The greatest compliment that was ever paid me was when one asked me what I thought and attended to my answer.
~Henry David Thoreau

Though many well-prepared speakers dread questions from the audience, Q and A should not stand for *quivering* and *agitated*! Allowing the audience to ask questions after your presentation is an excellent way to reinforce your message and to continue to sell your ideas. In addition, because listeners can ask for clarification, audience members are less likely to leave your presentation with misconceptions about your content. Because of these benefits, the question and answer period is vital to most speaking situations.

Here are some suggestions to more effectively handle the question and answer period.

Create the right mental set among your listeners by telling them early in the presentation that you will have a question and answer period. If you have an introducer, tell that person to mention your willingness to answer questions at the end of the presentation. People are more likely to ask questions if you tell them at the beginning that they will have this opportunity.

Show that you want queries. Say, "Who has the first question?" Look expectant after you ask for questions. Some of the enthusiasm for your presentation is lost if you have no questions from the audience, so you may have to "prime the pump." Say, "A question I'm often asked is...." Ask the question and then answer it. Steve's favorite question to ask himself is, "What President in your opinion was the most effective speaker of the 20th century?" Usually, "priming the pump" will motivate audience members to ask questions. If there are then no questions, you can finish with "What other question do you have?"

> *Q and A should not stand for quivering and agitated!*

When you do get a question, look at the person asking the question and repeat it, both for the sake of the audience and to give you a moment to think. By repeating the question you also insure that you understood what the person asked. However, do not continue looking at the person once you start to answer the question. Remember that you are still in a public speaking situation and that the whole audience should hear your answer—not just the person who asked the question. In addition, continue to stand where you are centrally located. Avoid the temptation to move directly to the person who asked the question because visually this will make the rest of the audience feel left out. As you end your answer, look back at the person and his or her facial expression will tell if you answered the question satisfactorily.

A little boy asked his mother a question and she responded, "Why don't you ask your dad?"

The little boy said, "I really didn't want to know that much about it!" You don't want the reputation his father had—that any question generates a long-winded answer.

Keep your answer concise and to the point. Don't give another speech. The audience will be bored if you take too long to answer a question. In addition, possibly the only person interested in the answer is the one who asked the question! If you can answer with a "yes" or "no," then do so. This keeps the tempo moving and will help keep the audience's attention. Even when you are asked an open-ended question, try to have a 30-second or less response. If need be, tell the questioner that you are glad to talk in greater detail after the program is over.

One of the toughest challenges is how to handle the loaded question. Simply solved: do not answer a loaded question, but unload it before you answer. Instead of answering a question such as, "What are you doing with all the money you are making from increased prices?" defuse it by saying, "I understand your frustration with the recent rate increase. I believe what you are asking is, 'Why such an increase in rates?'" Then answer that question. Allowing yourself to answer a loaded question will only end in argument. If the person is not satisfied with the changing of the question's wording, tell him or her that you will be glad to discuss the issue following the question and answer period and move quickly to the next question. If you give this response, remember to stay afterwards to talk to the questioner. Work hard not to lose your temper with someone who is trying to make you look bad by the question asked.

> *If no question is asked, "prime the pump" by asking a question and answering it.*

Sometimes you will have a listener raise his or her hand, but instead of asking a question that person will make an extended comment—or a speech. A way to handle this is to watch the person's speaking rate, and when he or she takes a moment for a breath interrupt with "Thanks for your comment....Next question?" Look to the other side of the room, and the long-winded speaker is not sure whether you interrupted or whether you really thought he or she was finished. Do not allow the person to continue with the "speech" because other audience members will lose the opportunity to ask questions.

Don't evaluate questions. Avoid saying "That was a great question," or "Good question." If the next person asks a question and you give no positive adjective, then it may seem that you did not approve of the question and that could stifle others from asking questions. If you want to affirm a specific question, simply say, "Thanks for asking that question." Another factor may be involved; as one sage said, "When someone says, 'That's a good question,' you can be sure it's a lot better than the answer you're going to get."

> *Never be afraid to say "I don't know."*

Consider concluding your speech after the question and answer period. This technique allows you to control the end of your time in front of the audience. Instead of the last question, the audience receives your prepared and planned conclusion. Begin your Q and A by saying, "Before I make some concluding remarks, who has the first question?" Then when you have completed the designated time for the question and answer period, go back to your conclusion. Thus you can end in a positive and upbeat way rather than trailing off with "So if there are no further questions, I guess that's it...."

Always maintain control of the speaking situation. When you open your presentation for audience participation, you risk losing control. Anticipate the unexpected. Plan ahead as much as possible. Look at your content and think about questions the audience is likely to ask. Prepare your own questions to ask. Thinking of questions may give you insight as to what to add to your content. As Jim Rohn said, "If you've reached the point in life where you feel you have all the answers you had better start asking some different questions."

Don't be afraid to say, "I don't know," and move on to the next question. (You might add that you will be glad to get back to them with an answer at a later time. Be up front with a questioner if you think the question is not relevant and in a kind way say so. Your response might be, "Actually, that question doesn't the fit the context of our discussion. Someone else might be able to answer that for you at another time."

Use the question and answer period to evaluate the content of your speech. If you are asked several questions about areas you think you covered, this may mean that you were not clear about certain explanations. Rethink how you might cover the material to be more easily understood. If you receive questions in areas you did not cover, that may mean you should add content the next time that will include answers to those questions.

Including a question and answer period can add risk to your presentation because you never know the direction the audience's questions will take. With the suggestions in this chapter, you can avoid most problems in your Q and A. Developing an engaging and lively question and answer period will help you end on a positive and enthusiastic note.

Pay Attention to Getting Better Even When You Are Good

Every day I get up and look through the Forbes list of the richest people in America. If I'm not there, I go to work.
~Robert Orben

A s an accomplished speaker, you are familiar with the basics, from preparation to practice to presentation. But even a good speaker can improve. One signal that you need a break from delivering speeches or you need new material for the next presentation is when your thoughts are about getting through the material or how boring this report is for the tenth time.

As we discussed in Chapter 4, "Pay Attention to Your Audience," you may have become self-centered again. A clue that you may be regressing is if, in the middle of your speech, you ask yourself, "I wonder how well I am doing?" The answer is probably in the negative because you have forgotten your audience.

Another hint is if you have a severe case of stage fright for no apparent reason. This may be a time to monitor your preparation time—a lack of preparation usually increases anxiety. You may be easily distracted from your audience during the presentation by the noise of plates or someone who is talking outside the room. Anytime you start thinking of self instead of your audience, it may be time to go back to the basics of speaking.

Certainly experience is important in becoming a more effective speaker. The more times you speak the more effective you will become. But to make the most of experience, work hard to do things which make you audience-centered. This will help you progress more quickly to the experienced speaker stage.

Another way of improving is to know you have more information than you can cover in the time allotted. A powerful presentation is one that comes from the overflow.

You are getting better with content when you say, "How am I going to cover all that I want to cover?" instead of "I hope I have enough material to take up the time I have to speak," Granted, finding an abundance of information can be challenging. When you have to eliminate rather than try to stretch some of your material, however, you are more likely to strengthen your speech with the most powerful examples, statistics, and testimony to prove your points.

One way to speak from your overflow is to incorporate a variety of sources. The more different sources you have, the more possibilities there are for materials to use in the presentation. For example, if you have an article from a trade journal, a quotation from a newspaper, and a quotation from a respected expert, you probably have more material on a single point than you can use; you will have to choose only one or two items. This scenario usually ensures rich and powerful pieces of evidence for that part of the presentation.

Make your reading and listening experiences a time of preparation. If you always have your mind open to materials related to the areas you speak about, you will be more likely to pick up new and creative material for your presentations.

> *A powerful presentation is one that comes from the overflow.*

For example, it was on vacation in Utah that we stayed in a bed and breakfast with hummingbirds feeding in the flower-covered front yard. Their energy, speed, and beauty impressed Steve. He began thinking, *How can I work what I am seeing into one of my speeches?* By simply having this on his mind, his awareness level regarding hummingbirds escalated; he read numerous books about hummingbirds and determined how to use them in illustrations.

Audiences know when you are speaking from the overflow. Your confidence and the depth of your material are obvious. Freshwater springs are often surrounded by plant and animal life because they provide an environment for growth. A presentation which springs from the overflow of the speaker's presentation provides the same environment of growth for listeners and is not soon forgotten.

If you have the opportunity to tell the same stories to difference audiences, you can continue to improve by memorizing your stories and practicing so they don't sound memorized. Write out your story and edit carefully. Writing the story insures excellent word choice and conciseness in the telling of the story. Practicing the story using gestures and movement to complement the content will make you an even more powerful storyteller. Practice the story in conversation with friends at dinner or at coffee so you can get audience feedback. Practice also gives you a better sense of how long you will need to tell the story.

Turn the sound down on the television set and watch the gestures and body movement of Jay Leno or David Letterman as they do their monologues. Concentrate on their nonverbal communication. This can give you ideas on improving your own delivery style. Notice the specific gestures they use. Look at their facial expressions as they speak. Observe how they use the stage from which they speak. Watch posture. Take note of how often they take steps. Consider how they connect with the audience through the nonverbal.

Video part or all of your next presentation and watch it in the privacy of your office or home. Pause the action two or three times to observe in more detail your delivery. You may find minor mannerisms that inhibit the overall effectiveness of your presentation. These you can easily correct. Listen to your rate of speech and the articulation of the words you use. You may find places where you run words together and determine how to articulate those more clearly.

> *Mute the sound on the television to watch the gestures and body movement of late night talk show hosts as they do their monologues.*

When a woman Steve was coaching saw herself speaking, she not only changed some of her speaking habits, but she disposed of the outfit she was wearing and went on a diet. You might not go to that extreme, but whatever changes you make will be significant to your effectiveness.

Develop your speaking vocabulary, incorporating words that paint vivid word pictures. Find synonyms which express your idea more succinctly or more positively. For example, a "challenge" is a better word than a "problem;" or the senior citizen "shuffled" across the room instead of "walked." The Visuwords™ Online Dictionary or Rodale's *The Synonym Finder* are excellent sources for alternate wording. Listen to your recording for words you overuse or misuse and make adjustments. Read books looking for descriptive words that might fit your oral style and incorporate them. Routinely look up the meaning of any word you don't know; sign up online for the Merriam-Webster "Word of the Day." In the process you will gradually improve the quality of your speaking vocabulary.

Read aloud to anyone who will listen. Read children's books, poetry, description or dialogue from your favorite current novel. Doing so will allow you to articulate syllables as well as increase your vocal variety. Small children are captivated by adults reading with animation their favorite Aesop's fable or Grimm's fairy tale. Practice different levels of volume and rates of speech. Or simply read aloud instead of silently when no one is around. Punctuation on the page will remind you of the need to use your voice as punctuation when you are speaking.

When an excellent speaker was called on to read a Bible passage in Sunday class, another class member commented, "Now that boy can *read*!" All he did that was out of the ordinary was articulate clearly and use vocal variety to enhance the meaning of the passage.

Watch movies that have speeches in them. Examples to choose from include Aaron Eckhart in *Thank You for Not Smoking,* Mel Gibson in *Braveheart*, Jack Nicholson in *A Few*

Good Men, and Gregory Peck in *To Kill a Mockingbird*. The movie context seeks to imitate a real speaking situation and you can pick up on nuances from the actors that you can incorporate in your own style of speaking.

Be especially sensitive to the audience's response to your content. Identify the specific parts of your speeches that continually command excellent attention or chuckles. Note when the "light bulb" goes on in their minds as shown by their facial expressions. After each speech, check off on your outline what went really well and what did not go well. Keep track over time. Analyze how you can improve on the weaknesses, or leave those parts out. Remember the adage, "If you're not keeping score, then you're just practicing."

> *The effective speaker wants to keep improving and moving to the next level of expertise.*

Ask a colleague or friend to observe and give feedback on a presentation you deliver. You might even have specific aspects of the presentation you want him or her to note and react to. Often people who are familiar with your one-on-one communication skills can provide input on how you can use certain speaking techniques more effectively.

The outstanding experienced presenter is never satisfied with her or his skill level, but is always seeking ways to improve. These suggestions can help take you to your next level of expertise. To the dedicated speaker, the best speech is always the next one!

You will learn a lot on Steve's website at www.sboyd.com. There you can subscribe to our free email communication newsletter and get insightful articles on improving your speaking and listening skills.

At www.sboyd.com you can also get information about:

- Humorous/Motivational Speeches
- Presentation Skills Workshops
- Individual Coaching
- Listening Seminars
- Retreat Speakers
- Interpersonal Communication Training
- Writing to Publish

From the website you can order:

- *Attention! The Art of Holding Your Audience in the Palm of Your Hand*
- *He Knows My Song and Other Devotionals to Challenge and Inspire*
- *Boyd's Benchmarks*
- *From Dull to Dynamic: Transforming Your Presentations*
- Laminated Listening Tips Cards
- Laminated Speaking Tips Cards

Lanita's website is www.lanitaboyd.com where you'll find updates on her speaking and writing.

To order products or find out more about programs on improving spoken or written communication, listening, parenting, or spiritual leadership, call Steve or Lanita toll-free at 800.727.6520, or email us at info@sboyd.com or lanita@lanitaboyd.com .

INDEX